T0329071

CROSSING BORDERS
-
IN AFRICAN LITERATURE

Smith and Ce [ed.]

AFRICAN
Library of Critical Writing

CROSSING BORDERS - in African Literature
Smith and Ce (Ed.)

©African Library of Critical Writing
Print Edition
ISBN:978-9-7837-0360-5

All rights reserved, which include the rights of reproduction, storage in a retrieval system, or transmission in any form by any means whether electronic or recording except as provided by International copyright law.

For information address:
Progeny (Press) International
Attn: African Books Network
9 Handel Str.
AI EBS Nigeria WA
Email: handelbooks@yandex.com

Marketing and Distribution in the US, UK,
Europe, N. America (Canada),
and Commonwealth countries by

African Books Collective Ltd.
PO Box 721
Oxford OX1 9EN
United Kingdom
Email: orders@africanbookscollective.com

Contents

Introduction

AN all-expansive heritage within and beyond regional or national groupings is built upon the framework of twentieth century black cultural nationalism as a consistent element of Africa-centred modernity which has seen modern African artists direct their investigation of black humanity toward the restoration and repair of past and the consequences of colonialism and westernisation. Against the consequent corruption and devaluation of tradition by imperial cultures, 'Crossing Borders' showcases intellectual attempts to commit the process of African interrogation of postcoloniality and postmodernity to the exploration of perspectives on black identities and the interaction of contemporary cultural expressions beyond the borders of Africa and across the Atlantic.

We have particularised on theoretical and critical perspectives that reveal how the continued and controversial influence of westernisation of Africa occasions a discontinuity in forms of life throughout the continent and now demands remedial visions and counteractive propositions to the cycle of abuses and fragmentation of the continent. Our studies of emerging and older works of African artists reveal how the African experience of modernity associated with the western paradigm is fraught with corruption and tensions at various political, social, economic and psychological levels of individual, communal and national existence.

The scholars in this volume have distilled some very significant historic and informative insights on modern African and black literary traditions. Through their research efforts, a new black consciousness is again being methodically espoused to articulate the greater unity and higher prospects in the diversities, fusions and hybridism that are embedded in the external and subjective realities of the universe. Here then are truly original perspectives on the art and writings of Africa which deign to interpret past histories, revaluate the present and adumbrate possibilities of Africa's cultural endowment to human development.

CS and CC

Chapter 1

Global Flows

AG Roy

THE global flows of Hindi popular cinema, christened
Bollywood by the global media, have largely been
located within the cultures of circulation that dominate
the contemporary global process. Bollywood is situated
in a transnational network of production, distribution and
consumption in the globalized economy in which local
cultures, repackaged and redirected in metropolitan hubs,
are made available for the consumption of the global
consumer. While this might be true of certain kinds of
films produced in the present phase of Hindi cinematic
history that may be defined as Bollywood, it does not
account for more 'local' films in Hindi with a significant
viewership within India and in Indian diasporas in the
present or the past. This narrative of Bollywood's
contemporary global flows to white audience in Europe,
North America, Canada and Australia occludes pre-
global travels of Hindi popular cinema to the Middle
East, Russia, China, Southeast Asia and Africa since the
1950s and those to Indian indentured populations in Fiji,
West Indies and Mauritius even earlier. Studies by Manas

Ray and Vijay Mishra on the popularity of Hindi cinema in Fiji, and by Vijay Devadas in Malaysia, have uncovered an older history of Bollywood's exhibition in Indian diasporic settlements and the incorporation of Bollywood images into Hindu epic narratives of Mahabharata and Ramayana on which diasporic desire converged in producing nostalgic myths of returns. Manas Ray's thesis in his pathbreaking essay on the centrality of Hindi cinematic texts to the production of diasporic Indian identities in Fiji is corroborated by Vijay Mishra in his book Bollywood Cinema: Temples of Desire. While Ray points out that Bollywood's identity producing function is retained by 'twice-migrant' Fiji Indians to Australia,1   Vijay Devadas's new work focuses on the forms of sociality that Bollywood texts perform in places of settlement through case studies from South-east Asia.

Despite the long history of Hindi cinematic flows to Africa, the researcher is forced to depend on anecdotal evidence to testify to the popularity of Hindi films in Africa. Shyam Benegal's mention of the influence of Mother India (1957) on the Ethiopian filmmaker brought the Hindi films' African constituency to public attention. Shashi Thaoor supports Benegal's statement through the example of his Senegalese friend's non-literate mother who would take a bus to Dakar to watch every Bollywood film despite not knowing a word of Hindi. But it is Brian Larkin's work on the impact of Hindi films on non-South Asian communities such as the Hausa of Nigeria that inaugurates a new direction in the study of Bollywood's African 'invasion' through connecting the movements of Hindi cinema in the past with Bollywood's transnational flows. More recent studies by Haseenah Ebrahim on South Africa confine themselves to Bollywood's circulation in the new global process However, new findings by Gwenda vander Steene in Senegal decouple Hindi cinema's pre-global circulation from diasporic settlement by examining cultural practices centred on Hindi cinematic texts in regions without a South Asian diaspora. This paper draws on these ethnographic studies to locate the global flows of Hindi cinema in these pre-global narratives of mobility to predate the history of globalization in Indian oceanic circulations, colonial migrations and post-colonial exchanges under the rubric of internationalization.

While Hindi films have been an integral part of the Indian diasporic experience, their popularity in many parts of the world without an Indian audience, as Larkin observed more than a decade ago, is an intriguing phenomenon. This undocumented history of Hindi cinema's popularity in both Anglophone and Francophone Africa was performed in a party at an autumn school on "Cultural Production and Conflict Mediation" organized by the African Studies Centre at the University of Bayreuth in October 1999 where creative persons from different African regions had congregated. Being a gathering of professional performers, the evenings invariably offered impromptu performances of poetry, music and dance. On one such evening, a young Nigerian theatre director and a celebrated Cameroonian actor collaborated to put together a song and dance sequence from a popular Hindi film of the late eighties.[2] Dressed in a salwar kameez borrowed from an Indian participant, the seasoned

Cameroonian stage actress imitated the inimitable jhatkas3 and matkas of the former reigning Hindi film queen Madhuri Dixit with consummate ease waving her duppatta as the young Nigerian director intoned the sounds of the chartbusting number aiji oji from the 1989 hit film Ram Lakhan while jumping about like Anil Kapoor. Their familiarity with the Anil Kapoor blockbuster of the late eighties confirms Janaki Nair's report in 2004 that "the regular matinee show in theatres in Senegal, Gambia, Cameroon and many other parts of Francophone Africa until recently was the Hindi film", a tradition that "has declined with the gradual disappearance of the old style theatres" (Npg).

A 'twice-migrant' Indian from Africa to New York recalls having watched Raj Kapoor's Mera Naam Joker 13 times in an open air theatre in Tanzania in the seventies.4 Her memories of viewing Hindi films such as Sangam (1964) and Mera Naam Joker (1970) constructed them as an integral aspect of family outings at which Indianness was staged through dressing up in ethnic outfits, eating Indian food and socializing with Indian friends. They corroborate Devadas's thesis about 'the social centrality' of viewing films through similar case-studies from Southeast Asia. But the New York theatre director makes a surprising revelation that connects Hindi films' African viewership to South Asian diasporic presence while removing it from the region of official statistics on the export and exhibition of films. She points out that while South Asians watched films seated within a fenced enclosure, Africans would view them from outside without being able to hear the dialogues.5 However, other memories, such as those of a Canadian academic of Ghanaian origin, reconstruct regular theatrical screenings of Hindi films in Ghana until the 1970s where he confessed to have watched Ramesh Sippy's Sholay (1975) after bunking school.6 The images made by a Vodun image maker in Benin interviewed by Dana Rush appear to have been inspired by calendars of Hindu gods and goddesses available in African owned shops. In the absence of insufficient fieldwork, anecdotal evidence of this nature must be pieced together to reconstruct the pre-global flows of Hindi cinema to Africa. And in the absence of official trade figures or records of state policies on film exports, such anecdotal details might help to explain how Tharoor's Senegalese friend's mother got addicted to Hindi films or the Ethiopian filmmaker derived inspiration from Mother India. The Hindi cinematic penetration into remote African regions appears to have been a combined effect of South Asian migration, quotas on film distribution and exhibition as well as an African desire of the Indian.

The global flows of Indian images to Africa must be framed against oceanic flows of images between Africa and India in contact zones of the past forged through travel and trade. Positing "the coastline of Benin Republic and Togo as a vortex, incorporating items and ideas from across the sea into its littoral", Dana Rush focuses on one such "vortextual phenomenon", that is, the incorporation of India via chromolithographic images (mostly Hindu) "into the eternally organic religious system of Vodun" (150). While the Vodun imagemaker Joseph Kossivi Ahiator, who incorporates Indian items into his own images, claims to have been inspired by his 'spiritual' journeys to India, Rush provides a rational explanation of the travels of Indian images to Africa through the arrival of chromolithographs to Africa as early as 1891 when the first colour reproductions were executed in Mumbai (Rush 59-60). The Vodun belief about Indian spirits being from the sea that Rush mentions unwittingly returns the movement of images in the present phase of globalization through advanced travel and communication technologies to the circulations of people in the Indian ocean dating back to the 14th century while connecting televisual flows to other visual practices. A return to these movements in a space without borders might prove to be educating in exploring the implication of living beyond borders. Pedro Machado in "Threads that Bind" traces the "multiplicity of long-term and complex networks of association across and around the ocean" and maintains that "an inter-relationship exists between cultural practices and material exchange".7 He shows how the historical spaces of South Asia and East, East Central and Southeast Africa were intimately connected through the cultural logics of cloth consumption and the circulation of networks of South Asian merchants. Machado's essay is remarkable in his detailed examination of the expanse of Gujarati vaniya networks in the eighteenth century and the determination of Gujarati textile patterns through the preferences of African consumers.

This transnational narrative of exchanges between Africa and India testifies to the contact zones of the past opened by travel, pilgrimage and trade through which cultural cross-fertilization occurred. However, in the absence of research on the history of this cross-fertilization, it is not possible to trace the process through which the idea of India was produced in the African imaginary. Studies in 2008 by Machado and Rush which identify specific cultural practices that emerged out of the oceanic exchange should go a long way in resolving the riddle of the similarity in textile patterns, visual and the musical production of India and Africa. As Rush's work shows, cinematic images are superimposed on earlier images such as those of the chromolithograph in the nineteenth century and those of producers by tales of travelers and slaves. Until more work such as that of Rush and Machado becomes visible, the history of African Indian cultural contact during the Indian oceanic trade must remain incomplete. However, it is possible to revisit the travels of Hindi cinema to Africa beginning in the 1950s through some recent essays.

"For over forty years, African audiences have been watching Hindi films" (Npg), Brian Larkin asserts, pointing out that generations of Hausa youth had grown up besotted with Bollywood and traced the influence of Bollywood fashions, music and stories on Nigerian cultural production. Larkin's ethnographic study of the appropriation of the Hindi cinema in the performance of, what he calls "a parallel modernity" by Hausa viewers throws light on its little known uses and gratifications. Vander Steene's 2008 fieldwork in Senegal builds on Larkin's pioneering work to disengage Bollywood's African viewership from the narrative of South Asian migration. In the same year, Haseenah Ebrahim adds a new dimension to the research on Bollywood audience by tracing the viewership from the ghetto to the mainstream in South Africa. The fieldwork by Fair, Larkin and vander Steene in Zanzibar, Nigeria and Senegal, respectively, testifies to the portability of Hindi cinematic narrative that lends itself to a wide variety of appropriations from providing a grammar for romance, lifestyles, fashions, and a model of values. Whether it is Hindi cinema's didactic function in Zanzibar or the performance of tradition or sacred in Nigeria, it appears quite clear that Hindi cinema's global flows even before the era of globalization have constituted a viable alternative to Hollywood. Yet their fieldwork which takes the Hindi cinema flows to Africa as axiomatic skims over the history of distribution and exhibition until the 1970s through which several generations of viewers were schooled in Hindi cinematic grammar.

Larkin's essays that frame the Bollywoodization of Bandiri music or Hausa videos against the discourse of globalization take the 50s flows for granted. As he states, "Hausa nostalgia for Indian films derives from their long historical popularity dating back to the 1950s, which has imprinted generations of northern Nigerians with the songs, narratives, and stars of Indian film" (100). Kano's appropriateness for the production of Bandiri music is reinforced by its being one of the major urban centres in which Hindi films were screened in the 50s and which later became the centre of a market of pirated CDs and DVDs. In another 1997 essay he points out that Indian films first imported by Lebanese cinema owners in the 1960s were the dominant film form in the North by the 1970s. Laura Fair corroborates Larkin's findings about the popularity of Hindi films in Africa through the example of Zanzibar where two thirds who watched films in the 1950s and 1960 named the same film Awara

(1951) as their favourite. Awara, the 1950s angst of unemployed youth in newly independent post-colonial states, connects the Raj Kapoor phenomenon in dissimilar post-colonial locations.

Studies of Hindi films in other parts of Africa such as Zanzibar or Senegal pick on Larkin's notion of parallel modernity to answer the question Larkin asked almost two decades ago: "What then, do African fans get from Indian movies?" (Npg). African preference for Bollywood melodrama to Hollywood finesse is a form of resistance to the western narratives of modernity. Larkin's term, 'parallel modernities', provides a memorable metaphor linking Bollywood effects to a postcolonial idiom of resistance. Through the evidence provided by these researchers, it appears that African identification with themes, characters and settings portrayed in Hindi films has as much to do with the identity of the post-colonial experience as with the desire for an alternative to western modernity. Zanzibari youth's identification with the angst of the unemployed youth in Awara, or of Zanzibari women's with the mother's struggle to raise her son mentioned by Fair, or the old or young in Nigeria whose identification with Mother India due to the strong visual, social and political similarities that Larkin refers to, all point to the replication of imperial policies formulated in one colony on the other due to which the mirrored concerns of the colony continue to shape the postcolony in the political, social as well as the personal space.

The idea of India that appears to have inspired a variety of activities in Africa ranges from the influence of Indian political movements on African resistance struggles, the conflict between tradition and modernity, and communal value systems. Underlying the incorporation of Indian visual, narrative and performative practices in a wide range of African cultural practices is the idea of India in which India becomes the signifier for a civilizational rhetoric that can be effectively juxtaposed against the west. In his analysis of the popularity of Hindi films in Africa, Larkin makes the important point that the narrative universe of the Hindi films is perceived as an alterity to the West through which indigenous Nigerian subjectivities might be performed. vander Steene's work on Indophiles in Senegal shows how Indophiles' viewing of Bollywood films and dancing to Bollywood songs is part of an ensemble of activities through which Indianness is performed.

The findings of Larkin, Fair, Steene reveal a Bollyphilia, often integrated into an Indophilia which is unexpected not only for its presence in areas without an Indian diasporic presence but for the similarity of the uses to which Bollywood is put within the nation and outside. As both Larkin and Fair show, the Hindi film song and dance convention offers an appropriate oblique medium for the expression of love in traditional societies where direct expressions of love are forbidden. The examples Fair provides of couples, both young and old, going to watch movies in theatres to perform romance carries nostalgic echoes to the subcontinent where movies and 'going to the movies' signified a realm of romance on which male and female desire for romance denied by society could be legitimately expressed. Similarly, the practice of repeat viewings at which Hausa viewers reproduced dialogues from the films, sang along to the tunes, and passed comments on the film narrative are no different from that of North Indian men going to watch movies as reported by Steve Derne. Finally, the absorption of Bollywood motifs, images and tunes not only in the African secular but also the sacred as in Bandiri songs which use Bollywood tunes to sing praises to the Prophet is striking for its resemblance to similar appropriations in India. While Larkin and Fair focus on the pull of Hindi films of the 1950s to 1980s as a traditional idiom among a predominantly non-elite audience, vander Steene and Ebrahim bring to light the emergence of Bollywood as 'Kool' among the elite audience in Senegal and South Africa. The integration of Hindi films in the African socio-cultural imaginary by a heterogeneous African audience extends Devadas' argument about the forms of sociality performed by cinematic practices in South Asian diasporas to other postcolonial settings while raising important issues about the transnationalization of a cinema produced as a national text.

If the Hindi film underpinned by a nationalist ideology produced the nation, as Sumita Chakravarty, M Madhava Prasad and others have convincingly argued, its transnational appropriations not only by the South Asian diaspora but also a non South Asian audience in the production of their own difference from the west invite rethink on the efficacy of the national framework for analyzing practices embedded in transnational flows. The presumed homogeneity of Larkin's Hausa and Fair's Zanzibari audience predicated on their shared Bollyphilia conceals the heterogeneity of Hindi cinema's diverse audience and the forms of sociality it performs in diverse settings. The fact that both Larkin and Fair's audience are Muslim and proletariat as opposed to vander Steene's and Ebrahim's elite multicultural audience provides an important lead to the conceptualization of cinematic flows to Africa. It is also significant that in their appropriation of parallel modernities, African communities in Larkin, Fair and vander Steene return to the Hindi films from the 1950s to 1980s.

The surprising convergence of Muslims not only in Africa but also in South and Southeast Asia and the Middle East on Hindi cinematic texts largely structured by Hindu religious practices points to syncretic religious, political and cultural formations produced through oceanic exchanges in the past. The title of Fair's essay, "Making Love in the Indian Ocean", calls attention to these pre-national translocal movements through which remote cultures came into contact with one another. The unproblematic amalgamation of Hindu, Muslim and Sikh practices into the syncretic cultures and religions in the past that persisted at the village level until the end of the nineteenth century was marked by a closure with the emergence of Islamic, Hindu and Sikh nationalisms thereafter.

After the thickening of boundaries following the Indian partition of 1947, Hindi cinema emerged as the boundary crossing space in which the cultural syncretism through which the Persian qisse and dastan were integrated into the Indian narrative and performing arts was retained. These syncretic formations were produced through the trade on the oceanic as well as caravan routes tracing a history of cultural continuity from Africa to India across the Perso-Arabic kingdoms that survives in

24

Hindi cinema and lends itself to reappropriation by dispersed ethnic groups in the present. While they have been co-opted in the propagation of a nationalist ideology, the narrative and aesthetic basis of Hindi cinema in this syncretic tradition explains why African audience are able to identify with their thematic conflicts despite their religious difference.

Larkin's pioneering work which throws new light on the forms of sociality performed by Bollywood films sells itself short in its framing of the argument against the new model of global flows for describing practices that are informed by the pre-global exchanges of the fifties. The discrepancy in Larkin's work is typical of the new studies that celebrate the globalization of Bollywood cinema insensitive to the multiple histories and geographies of cultural flows. The flows of Hindi cinema that defy both the national rubric of South Asian film scholars as well as the transnational framework deployed by diasporic researchers must be differentiated with respect to region, ethnicity, period and generation. However, the different phases of flows of Hindi films—prenational, national and postnational—converge on the transnational viewership of Hindi films. The function of Hindi films as sites for the production of diverse ethnic and national identities through audience identification with the narrative conflicts and motifs complicates the framework of national cinema within which early studies examined the Hindi film.

It would appear that Hindi films that were underpinned by nationalist ideologies produced a portable national text capable of being reproduced in other postcolonial locations and co-opted in the production of other national identities. As Larkin demonstrates, the binary of tradition and modernity through which India and the west is reproduced in the Hindi film accounts for its portability in other locations where Indian traditional values acquire a centrality in the resistance to westernization. The tradition-modernity binary that film scholars have located as the narrative centre of the cinematic conflict within a complex network of familial relations that becomes the framework within which national questions are posed in the Hindi film has an immense appeal for developing societies at the cusp of tradition and modernity.

Since most studies of Bollywood's popularity in Africa refer to cinematic texts of the 50s and 60s rather than films produced after the insertion of Hindi cinema into the circuits of global capitalism, their illustration of global cultural flows complicates the narrative of globalization. The media flows of globalization riding on advanced travel and communication technologies intersect with the earlier waves of the travels of Hindi films to Africa to produce heterogeneous audience. Their absorption of Hindi cinematic vocabulary from the 1950s to the 1970s when Hindi films were screened in theatres to the late eighties when they were circulated by video libraries and the present multiplex viewing contexts cannot be equated due to the transformation of the proletarian audience of Hindi cinema to Bollywood audience.

In contrast to the universal appeal of Hindi films until the 1970s when they were screened in theatres and formed the sole form of entertainment in Nigeria, the video boom encouraged an informal economy of distribution independent of state intervention but also bifurcated the viewership into the elite, anglicized viewers of Hollywood films and the non-elite, indigenous speakers of African languages. Larkin's work is extraordinary in its detailed description of the subaltern cosmopolitanism of the pre-global era, which contrasts with the multiplex South Asian and non South Asian audience of Ebrahim's study. The survival of the Bollywood film in the era of globalization must be attributed to a similar pull of traditional family values in the face of the renewed threat to indigenous cultural values by the forces of global capitalism. Once again, African audience turn to Bollywood films to perform modernity to resist the homogenizing wave of globalization. The Bollywood arrival in Africa emerges from both the export of Hindi cinema to Africa in the 'nationalist' phase of the 1950s and the global flows of culture in the new cultures of circulation. The Bollywoodization of Hindi cinema cannot be understood without a reference to the transnational circulation of Hindi film in the nationalist era.

The problematic location of Hindi cinematic travels in different phases of transoceanic circulations raises important issues about the conceptualization of national cinemas as well as that of globalization. The celebration of Bollywood as a culture of globalization to illustrate the reverse flows from the non-west to the west must be juxtaposed against the long history of transnationalization through which Hindi cinematic texts were incorporated into African cultural practices to assume African ethnic or national identities. Attention to the difference between the subaltern audience of Hindi cinema in the past and the cosmopolitan consumers of Bollywood in the present also points to an alternative narrative of subaltern cosmopolitanisms through which cultural exchanges took place between ordinary folks in the process of trade and travel. The studies on the viewership of Hindi cinema in Africa help to recover these narratives of subaltern cosmopolitanism that have been erased by the euphoria over the elite cosmopolitanisms of the present global process.

Chapter 2

African Spaces, European Places

R Codling

THE negotiation for African spaces within Eurocentric places often transpires through the leaves of the African novel. The arguments of Keith Booker in terms of deconstructive literary thought, Father Placide Frans Temples, a proponent of Ethnophilosophy, Alexis Kagame on the African concept of 'Being' and John Mbiti on the African concept of time are demonstrated in the inherent counter-cultural nature of the African novels of two contemporary writers, Aminatta Forna (*Ancestor Stones*) and Donato Ndongo (*Shadows of Your Black Memory*). Both works serve as responses to the Western canonical template of British and Spanish literature. Each chronicles the path of a heroic protagonist from assimilation into European culture to "repatriation to African identity or space" (Masolo 2).

The indigenous peoples of Sierra Leone, a long 'charge' or colony of the British Empire, and Equatorial Guinea, a long 'charge' of the Spanish Empire, were educated to revere and be faithful to the colonial 'Crown' sovereigns. Cultural imperialism is a carefully, crafted colonial mechanism to eradicate any semblance of merit in the manner in which indigenous people govern their lives. However, it was the arrogant 'thought' coupled with extreme naïveté of the European insurgents that misled them into perceiving that the physical conquest arrested native, ontological principles[1]. African ontological and cultural identity is not easily arrested. Only physically were the conquerors of Sierra Leone and Equatorial Guinea successful in shifting the axis of power from the native to the European. The offspring (Forna and Ndongo) of two 'conquered,' native peoples successfully retain definitive African spaces in the European places of England and Spain that they have migrated to. Thus one may construe that the early nurturing of the communalism of African thought or Ethnophilosophy, dormant during the formative years of the individual's colonization, may resurface in a post-colonial state of mind[2].

Similarly, the textual and metaphysical formats of the novels by Aminatta Forna and Donato Ndongo exhibit deconstructive tendencies in the manner in which they write. Whether writing in British English or Spanish, these authors bear evidence to the power. But the very genre of the African novel serves to disembowel colonist literary tendencies and philosophies and assume an independent position in the landscape of World Literature. *Ancestor Stones* and *Shadows of Your Black Memory* adhere to the formula of the African, not Western, novel. And Forna and Ndongo attest to the survival of ancestral, ontological identities that can only be attributed an African literary antecedent that defies the usurpation of Modernity. In essence, even within the confines of European domains, the styles and themes of these writers bear witness to the un-arrested traditions of the African novel.

The Examples of Ndongo and Forna

The role of history in the African novel is an integral one. This essential role of history within this genre may qualify its status as a literary element. For Donato Ndongo and Aminatta Forna, history forms the psychological landscape upon which the narratives take form. The historical religious and colonial politics in Equatorial Guinea become one of the main subjects of Ndongo's novel. Ndongo is bold in his political assertions throughout his novel.

Aminatta Forna's does utilize traditional, African literary devices, which act as a conduit for the progression of her characters and plot. She drapes the history of Sierra Leone beneath the mythical and metaphysical. In *The African Imagination* Abiola Irele sheds light upon the status of the narrative form in precolonial Africa. According to Irele, narrative forms of various registers were "integrated into the fabric of social life ...the oral mode ... [facilitating] an immediacy of response that went beyond the purely aesthetic to embrace the symbolic and the cognitive spheres of awareness" (104). Forna's use of allegory coupled with metaphors, similes, symbolism, personification remains consistent in this manner of the African model.

Most importantly, Forna relies heavily upon the literary element African Realism[12] also called "Complementary Realism"[13]. In a passage where the reader becomes introduced to the recollection of the 'girl' narrator, the reader readily accepts and submits to the company of a child and the world of African/Complementary Realism. Some aspects of this recollection of the narrator bear the attributes of the Fantastic, as illustrated by Tzvetan Todorov in *The Fantastic: A Structural Approach to a Literary Genre*. For the Fantastic defies reason and the reader's reality 'equilibrium.' No reference in Todorov's text is made to African Realism. Understandably, Todorov addresses the western canon. African Realism is simply African. This is the distinguishing factor that illuminates *Ancestor Stones* and places it in a non-Western genre. Forna's 'girl' narrator recalls her mother's words in this passage:

She [mother] pointed to the weaver birds darting in and out of their nests suspended from the branches of tree...And she told me the birds were the souls of all the children who had died....There were men whose skins were luminous as pale shadows of the moon when it dances across bare flesh...Men who sailed their houses across the sea and were so thin because they ate only fish and drank sea water. (Forna 23)

To 'be' a child is to accept without asking or questioning. Forna stresses this primary innocence in this passage—in terms of the mother's communicated lessons about birds and men. The child displays reverence and acceptance of such. The means that Forna uses to communicate myth and metaphor is with a slight infusion of the metaphysical, stemming from African Realism. Forna uses metaphors ("birds were the souls of children") and similes ("skins were luminous as pale shadows of the

32

moon"). For the European reader, the tale that the mother communicates is a mere story. But the story, within the context of African Realism, represents far more. The very story is symbolic of the union of the Sierra Leonean people with nature. In this manner, the narrative qualifies as an allegorical mission towards self identity. Masolo reviews the notion of "Language and Reality" in accordance with the philosophy of Alexis Kagame, an acknowledged scholar of Bantu languages. Masolo states:

The basic point that Kagame expresses is that concepts, and indeed whole world views, precede language. The structure and grammatical rules of language are modeled in agreement with the cosmological ordering of the universe. The modeling of linguistic structure in accordance with philosophy, according to Kagame, was done by the great ancestors – philosophers who were the sages of the tribe. (96)

Kagame may have studied the Bantu people but there are African universal lessons to be derived from his study. For instance, Forna's language and reverence for the role of mythology contains many cultural indicators universal to Africans. Her African viewpoint, as conveyed in the novel itself, lends itself to the belief that she is adhering to the wisdom and beliefs of her Temne people. The concepts of her African people, not Westerners, frame the linguistic structure of her words. Our narrator understands this as part of her ontological, African 'being.' These deliberations in the story may be construed as myth by Westerners, but the story may have a real purpose. Simply, the narrator's mother is teaching her daughter to be wary of things. A Western equivalent may be found in the adage: 'Everything may not be as it seems.' And to further address this issue, Forna writes of an important episode witnessed by the narrator Mariama involving her pious father and mother. The father wishes to eradicate any superstitious practices in his home:

That evening my father had interrupted my mother in her room, as she read her fortunes in the stones.... He demanded her stones.... My mother pleaded.... He threw up his arm. Scattered the stones to the stars.... A dark rock the shape of a man's cigar. A broken pebble, open like a split plum. A stone with a dimple that fitted my thumb. A twinkling crystal. A pale three cornered stone. ...The Ancestors she [mother] called them.... And now I recognize them for what they are. (56)

The narrator's pious, Islamic father wishes to abolish any remnant of superstition from his household. His wife, a fragile, tormented creature, wishes to retain her hold upon her pre-colonial, ancestral practices. In one swoop, the husband attempts to banish superstition from his home and his act traumatizes his fragile wife. Yet his act dramatizes the importance of the stones. The stones were the woman's link to her own spiritual, ontological being. Each stone, personified, was a female family member, each possessing the ability to recall the spirit of a particular family member. Ironically, the mysterious letter that appeared at the commencement of the novel possesses the (same) ability to recall the narrator, Abie, to her home. Forna's use of personification works well to demonstrate the essence of the connection between her ontological 'self,' nature, and her African ancestors. And proverbs, also, become a means of reflection within this text for expressing female perspectives regarding African space. Such is illustrated in the sayings:

1. "A marriage cannot be pulled apart easily as a dam in a river." (180)
2. "Who knows how much a pretty pair of shoes pinch, except the person wearing them." (218)
3. "Luck is like adjoining pools of water, each flowing into the other." (78)

Forna communicates the issues of 'female' space pertaining to African women in these proverbs of her female kin: (1) Marriage is a union of female and male and the "collective I" of the community. It cannot be put asunder easily in her culture. (2) Beauty is relative to the beholder in her culture. One may see the aesthetics, but not be in tune to the pain. (3) Luck is not spawned from a single source; it is brought about through the convergence of two or more entities. These types of proverbs or aphorisms are aspects of the classic, African novel. Inclusions such as this attest to the position of writers and critics regarding the fundamentals of the African novel as stemming from the oral culture of the people.

Donato Ndongo's African novel may have meant to be the start of an allegorical treatise. Monique Ngamba writes that this novel "is the first title of the trilogy *The Children of the Tribe*, which tells the story of a generation of Guineans through colonialism, independence, dictatorship, and the present in Equatorial

Guinea" (3). Ndongo adheres to a literary format in this narrative that incorporates allegory with imagery, internal and external (political) dialogue, and symbolism that flows in a pastoral scheme. This is the classical literary format of many African works such as Chinua Achebe's *Things Fall Apart* and D.O. Fagunwa's *Forest Of a Thousand Daemons*. Ironically, Nodongo's work is most similar to a fellow Equatorial Guinean attributed to writing *Cuando Los Combres Luchaban* or *When the Combes Fought*. The author of this work, Leoncio Evita, was successful in illustrating the customs of his Combe people during pre-colonial times (N'gom 33). Leoncio Evita's use of a pastoral scheme was most successful in communicating the role of nature in the lives of the Combe people of Equatorial Guinea in pre-colonial times. Specifically, Evita's own tragic protagonist, Roku, becomes embroiled in a conflict between native culture (Combe) and Modernity (represented by Brother John Stephen). A similar conflict exists between Ndongo's character Tio Abeso and the Catholic priest in his work. Tio Abeso represents the pre-colonial, 'Fang' native that reveres nature. And it is Tio Abeso that tutors the boy in *Shadows of Your Black Memory* through symbolic lessons regarding the union between man and nature. Tio Abeso says:

The alligator was one of the tribe's taboos, the most important one; he protected the chiefs and elders of your lineage, children and pregnant women also; he sheltered you from scheming demons and enemy spirits…. The alligator should be respected. It must not be touched. (83)

The young plebe learns to not fear, but respect, an animal that maintains the physical and spiritual 'ecosystem' of his people. The image of the alligator aids in illustrating the harmony between the Fang people and nature. Such a union between man and nature are symbolic of the partnership that both share. The elder reiterates that the 'ecosystem' must be maintained. Also, the elder warns that if this partnership is not maintained and respected, nature and man face doom. Later the boy asks what would happen if an alligator attacked his kinsmen. Tio Abeso informs him that such an act had occurred right before the white occupiers arrived. The attack itself was a harbinger of things to come and not an act of evil on the part of the alligator. Ndongo's focus upon this particular lesson offers an insight into the uncle's nurturing influence upon the narrator. The philosophy of the Spanish clergy did not embrace the notion of nature and man as being co-dependents. But Tio Abeso's lessons did prove to be enduring in the ensuing future of the adult nephew.

As earlier stated, Donato Ndongo's professional career has been greatly impacted upon by Chinua Achebe and his text *Things Fall Apart*[14]. It is no wonder that the village becomes a central point of focus for grooming and learning in *Shadows of Your Black Memory*. In a passage from Achebe's text, the tragic hero Okonkwo has committed an infraction during a holy period. The infraction that Okonkwo committed holds a threat which may cause disharmony with the goddess of the earth. Here are the words of the priest, Ezeani:

"Listen to me," he said when Okonkwo had spoken. "You are not a stranger in Umuofia. You know as well as I do that our forefathers ordained that before we should any plant crops we should observe a week in which a man does not say a harsh word to his neighbor. We live in peace with our fellows to honor our great goddess of the earth without whose blessing our crops will not grow. You have committed a great evil." (32)

Thus the young narrator of *Shadows of Your Black Memory* is guided by (his uncle) a renowned tribe elder in the same manner as Okonkwo in *Things Fall Apart*. There is a similar message communicated by the Equatorial Guinean elder and the Nigerian priest that one must revere nature or suffer the consequences. Donato Ndongo writes here, even in exile, from the African vantage point of the Fang, Equatorial Guinean villager.

While Aminatta Forna's novel, *Ancestors Stones*, was written (in exile) in England from the African vantage point of Temne, a Sierra Leonean villager, Ndongo, writes directly in Spanish and nothing obscures his voice through his 'persona,' his ontological self, and his extended 'self.' The novel qualifies as an allegorical mission because the experience is a symbolic journey in pursuit of African identity. The author's mission is to communicate the political identity of the 'you,' (Equatorial Guineans) in terms of anti-colonialism and the ensuing problems. Thus Ndongo's novel (internal) is an exercise that permits the author to address the political (external) important issues of his people. As he says:

"Las tiniebas de tu memoria negra" es para mi, un ejecico catartico, una doble interiorizacion, tendente a exorcizar a los "demonios" acumulados a lo largo de la pueblo guineano: las supersticiones, el colonialismo, el racismo inherent a la accion colonizadora y el provoca, como reaccion, en los colonizados... (qtd. in N'gom "La autobiografia" 73)

Ndongo provides the rationale for writing his novel stating that he wrote to exorcize the 'demons' (personally and for fellow Equatorial Guineans) of superstitions, colonialism and racism. Essentially, he seeks to achieve freedom from the restraints that hinder him and Equatorial Guinean people from being autonomous from the colonial powers. And in doing so, Ndongo aspires to reclaim Equatorial Guinea 'pre-colonial space.' Thus the narrator of *Shadows of Your Black Memory* renounces his own commitment to the Catholic Church and does not wish to seek the priesthood. This is a symbolic renunciation because it is very similar to Ndongo's political epiphany[15]. Ndongo's African 'being' seeks to assert itself over any religious fervor.

Ndongo provides his reader with equally valuable jewels of 'aphorism' which illustrate, as opposed to explain, the pre-colonial culture and the ethos of his people. Here are some examples:

(A) "...idleness is the mother of all vices" (65)
(B) "Family relations are like a nightingale caught in a trap; even as it rots, it will always be hanging by a vein." (93)

(C) "Power is above all pain, feeling what the governed feel, knowing how to endure...." (125)

Ndongo accents the African male issues of responsibility within 'Fang' space by incorporating the wisdom passed on by the elders in the sayings: (A) Idleness is the premier of all sins; (B) The family, the tribe, the community may be in decay but there will be a remnant of a link that forever ties them together; (C) True power is not glamorous; it is assuming the ailments of all within your charge, enduring and prevailing in spite of all. The true wisdom of Ndongo's people stems from another source that existed long before the Spaniards. His Uncle Tio had once declared to the priest:

We don't read books. We know our tradition because the eldest member passes it on to the young. This is how we have lived.... You say you have brought peace, but you were the ones who incited war.... The only problem that I see with you is that you want us to give up our customs and trust your ancestors. (92)

The narrator's uncle is adamant in his declarations regarding his people. They (the Fang people) do not need to read what was passed from one generation to the next. This was their life. Forna's writings support Kagame's views regarding the elders and the preeminence of the cosmic order of the universe over structural language (as observed by the Bantu). One might construe that in the case of Ndongo's text the great elders, Tio Abeso, for example, play a great role in Fang culture in making the same determinations.[16] Abeso would recall and bear witness to the survival of his people and his 'being' through his very recollection of these events. Retrospect, in terms of history and the reality of the present, is vital in the African novel.

Resolution in the African Novel

When one considers the Western literary notion of a 'resolution' it conflicts greatly with the concept as it exists in African literature. The classic African texts *Forest of a Thousand Daemons* by D. O. Fagunwa and *The Palm-Wine Drinkard* by Amos Tutuola do not come to a resounding, comforting halt during the last phase of the chronicle. Virgil's *Aeneid* and Homer's *The Odyssey* follow this tradition too. These Greek allegories summon the listener to prepare for another chapter to come. The stories of the African and Greek classics endure because the characters, the story, and the legacies, are enduring. Forna's *Ancestor Stones* follows the African tradition. Peter Parker offers an insight into the perpetual nature of the story and the legacy foretold in Forna's novel; he writes:

It is indeed the spirits of the individual women that were commemorated in the ancestor stones that give the book its title. Until outlawed under the new male-dominated religion, the stones were handed down from mother to daughter to be consulted in times of trouble. As a result of both the experiences and the limitations of the society in which they live, Forna's women endure life as much as they enjoy it, but one is left with a more cheering image of them in old age, survivors whose stories have been restored to them by the granddaughter who went away to become a writer. (1)

A further testimony to the survival of this 'elder culture' is found in the African ontological consciousness of the writer that produced the text itself. Aminatta Forna's novel, on the surface, descends to a predictable, traditional resolution following the introduction, rising action, climax, falling action, and finally the conclusion. There are, however, no predictable moments in Africa or Sierra Leone. In the latter chapters of *Ancestor Stones* the tempest of contemporary Sierra Leone invades the metaphysical world of Forna and her family. Political reality ensues and the imagery of Forna's text becomes dark. She writes:

I saw them returning at night, moving between the headstones and the mausoleums, indistinguishable from the shadows, from the dark shapes of the statues. Great slabs of stone and marble were heaved aside, coffin lids swung open. I saw the graves open up, the spirits of the dead walk away from their resting place....That was how they got into the city, wasn't it? The rebel army. They hid their weapons and their men in the graveyards. Collected them at night. (305)

Here African Realism combines with African political reality. The phantoms of the night are seen in a vision that is more real than supernatural. Forna realizes in this passage the decline of the 'collective I' of Sierra Leone. Ndongo suffers a similar sense of loss in the latter segment of his novel. He reflects upon his Equatorial

Guinean people from a detached standpoint. The war in Sierra Leone ravaged the culture, the people and their beliefs. The rebel soldiers, some mere children, hid their weapons (tangible and human) in graveyards, desecrating the dead and the holy. Nothing was sacred, so much so that Forna alludes to the fact that even the dead fled their resting places to escape the anarchy. But Forna finds redemption for her culture and her people through the resilience of her aunts. They defy the chauvinistic males in a purely chauvinistic society for most of their lives. The battles of men could never prove them 'un-done.' Pacing to a slow closing of events, the narrator says:

In the meantime certain giddiness had come over my aunts as if the time spent remembering the girls and women they had once been invigorated the spirits. They lifted the past from their own shoulders and handed it to me. I didn't see it as a burden, not at all. Rather a treasure trove of memories of lives lived and lessons learned, of terrors faced and pleasures tasted.... Still today and every day those women appear to me in my mind's eye... (315)

The ontological union of Forna's identity with those of her 'kinswomen' is complete. She sees her aunts clearly: past, present, and future. That which has separated has been rejoined in terms of the Sierra Leonean society too. Perhaps all of this is due to the fact that Forna has served her purpose as a griot of her kinswomen. Forna obtains much of the legacy of her kinswomen through orality which she transfers to the written word. Griots, according to Irele, are part of a special category of individuals known as guardians of the word and 'fathers of the

43

secrets'....and the griot is the embodiment in every sense of the word (11). The term griot suits Forna well. The immediate spaces which once divided Forna and her ontological 'self' dissipate. The conflict between the narrator's African space and the European place are arrested as a result. Forna chooses to have the African space of her narrators in *Ancestor Stones* prevail with the ancestors. This is the major underlying theme. The five narrative voices are indistinguishable, at times, because they are, in fact, indistinguishable. This is the 'collective I' philosophy of Africa or, as Irele avers, "one that is properly commensurate with a sphere of existence and an order of experience that, by the fact of their being rigorously circumscribed, conduce to its institutional strength" (121).

The voices of the female narrators certainly act as a collective entity and strength. The 'musical accompanist', known as Abie, eventually fades from of view. But upon reaching the novel's closing stage, all of the narrative voices reach a 'crescendo.' And Abie is no longer required to accompany: they become one voice. For this accomplishment, Abie earns her 'space' among, not aside, the voices. Henceforth, she is in union with her space as a Sierra Leonean:

On my way through the village people called out little courtesies to one another and me: 'Did you sleep well?' And I replied: 'Thanto Kuru.' I was no longer a stranger. I knew just where into all of this I fitted. Because in this small world everybody had a place, meaning they all knew how they came to be there. A story of which every detail was cherished. And I had mine. (314)

Forna illustrates her full integration into her Sierra Leonean space and community in this passage and freely relinquishes her hold upon her 'persona.' This passage cites her passing through the village not as a guest; she is now a full-fledged community member. No longer is she in exile from her identity; no longer stranded in a European place. Her identity is fully realized through the recognition of the community. The story itself, her story too, of the women of her family finally weaves into a cloth of which she is a vital part. This is the author's personal denouement. Thus the four women and the narrator become one. Later, in London, after fully discarding the cloak of her 'persona,' Forna writes:

I am writing this at my desk in the den. In front of me sits a bowl of stones, a gift to me from Mariama along with the one she gave me in Rofathane (the family plantation that she inherited)....My daughter loves to play with them while I write and she waits for a moment of my attention. In her hands they rustle and click against one another.... 'Listen' she beckoned me down. I lowered my head to join her. 'What is it?' 'Listen to the noise they make,' she replied. 'It sounds like they're talking.' (173)

Now the stones have been passed to another generation. Forna's own daughter is engaging her ancestors in same fashion as her female elders before. Ontologically, the passing of this stone 'heritage' to another generation solidifies Forna's absorption into her

African community, the negotiation of her African space and identity now completed.

Ndongo's journey finds closure in a different manner. Michael Ugarte, the translator of Ndongo's *Shadows of Your Dark Memory* into English reflects upon the work in his own *Translator's Postscript*. Ugarte says: "Clearly, along with the vicissitudes of identity and race construction, Ndongo's lasting concern in his fiction has been colonialism and the "dark idea" – as Joseph Conrad called it in *Heart of Darkness*" (168). This is undeniably true; Ndongo has remained true to the original (political) format with *Shadows of Your Dark Memory* the first installment within a trilogy series[15]. The story of the Equatorial Guinean people does not end with the last page of *Shadows of Your Black Memory*. Ndongo desires to display more to communicate more. Showcasing the culture of the Equatorial Guinean people was secondary to the political premise of this text. Ndongo's narrator seeks to redeem himself (and his people) from their colonial, Eurocentric aspirations. The resolution of the novel comes as a result of a heightened sense of ontological awareness of the original sin of colonial aspirations. Evidence of such is found in the 'confessional,' narrative tone of the latter chapter. In an attempt to seek atonement the narrator laments as he reflects back upon his departure from Equatorial Guinea:

When you all met father Ortiz at noon at the mission, you didn't know that many, many years would pass before you would again walk on that beach, a beach with bubbling waters…. The blacks conquered by the will of the planters were gathered there with boxes, sacks, packages, wood, themselves determined to initiate a life as conquers... (152)

The narrator looks back with remorse and guilt. Yet he does not realize the profound significance of that moment in time. Seared in the mind's eye, now, are the images of the fellow Equatorial Guineans also departing from their cultural base. Ndongo explores the universe of alienation of the colonized as it applied to Equatorial Guinea being transformed to Guinea Espanola. He did not understand, nor did his people, that they were leaving, departing from the base of their culture and people forever. Instead, they were eager to be like the conquerors. The narrator is 'intoxicated' by the image of himself "...return[ing] many years later, carrying the wisdom and the power of the whites, determined to be the new boss in town... a replica of Father Ortiz..." (153). He does not realize that his success would stem from the absolute alienation from his cultural identity.

Within the *Shadows of Your Black Memory*, there is one truth: The narrator and his kinsmen are seduced. The planters/colonists disinherit the people of their own land and culture. The promises of good pay, fine women and drink are false. The narrator and his kinsmen are lured to false paradises that would only rob them of their cultural identity. In the end Ndongo's persona and his kinsmen would share a meager lot because... "just like *you*", he says, "...they would break their backs on plantations and *you* would genuflect at the altar, initiated into the white man's practice of witchcraft...." (152).

With the bitter, the narrator, in retrospect, accepts the sweet. Yes, there is the loss, the death of something precious never to be regained. But there is something just as valuable retained. That which was disinherited impacted upon all of the Equatorial Guinean people. But in sharing the loss, Ndongo's narrator and 'persona' bond with the people. The union of the 'collective I' and 'collective you' is complete for the narrator of *Shadows of Your Black Memory* and his people. This retrieval and emersion of the narrator's ontological and African 'self' is similar to the union that takes place in the final segment of *Ancestor Stones*. Ndongo's narrator and his Fang people are united by the rhythm of music and the motion of tide sweeping them together, away. Forna's own protagonist finds redemption and salvation in the fraternity of her aunts. Ndongo's own protagonist sees the music of his people as the unifying factor. And although the Equatorial Guineans are being swept away, they are still together and bound by the intangible. They were one people in pre-colonial times, colonial times, and Modernity. Ndongo's narrator finds the music of his homeland to be as eternal as the people themselves. The guitarist's rhythms serve to resonate eternally, confirming the perpetuation of Fang culture.

Aminatta Forna and Donato Ndongo find their African ontological existence even within a physical, European space through the development of an indigenous African literary tradition. Thus the scheme of an African novel can be defined only in the artist's term of 'local color.' The African writer or artist uses the template to direct his own focus of color that actually incorporates his/her African identity and ontological space. Each writer or artist distinguishes himself/herself in the manner of the 'arc' or literary plot in which the color is to be displayed.

The ontological spaces of African writers are the result of the African 'oral' traditions which define time, creation, ethics, and nature of the tribe as a member of the 'collective', not individual, 'I' of Africa and Africans. The teachings of the elders may only appear dormant during vast periods of colonization and displacement but writers such as Forna and Ndongo offer an illustration of what Aimee Cesaire had referred to as a 'repatriation of African identity' and the reclaiming of the 'original space.'

Chapter 3

African and AmerIndian Epistemologies

M de la Cruz-Guzmán

THE Visitor and *Shell Shaker* are primary African and American-Indian texts that employ the concept of bi-living to redefine human individual and collective existence from the borderland of indigenous time and space. In the liminal spaces between and among coeval realities the protagonists achieve an open experience −and an understanding− of the confluence of life in multiple realities (both temporal and spatial) and the state of the indigenous person in coeval space-time. Thus with bi-living, the colonial grand narrative of the African savage in need of European civilization, the post-modernist counter-narrative of a liberated post-independence failure, and the indigenous postcolonial, or rather, beyond-colonial, narrative of ancestral oversights, can be processed together so that the interconnections and the understanding of indigeneity, the denigrating western mythology about it, and its potential application for positive change can all be seen clearly in this borderland.

By this fictional development Ce and Howe provide an opening for integrating the indigenous self without DuBois's double consciousness, Fanon's inferiority complex, or Ngugi's decolonized mind. Their concept of bi-living creates the possibility of a healthy indigenous mind and psyche fully aware that it is in this multiple existence that "the past is, or can be, a personal experience of the present, not its nostalgic recovery…not lost innocence but integrated wisdom, the unity of the tree of knowledge and the tree of life" (150) as Quijano notes in "Modernity, Identity, and Utopia in Latin America."

In *The Visitor* Ce masterfully integrates the possibilities of indigenous bi-living in the on-going existence of the main character Mensa/ Deego/ Erie, inserting hope and, also, rejecting the failure trope faithfully meted out by Western media, politics, and neo-colonialism. In this ground-breaking novel, bi-living brings the triad of a single character to wholeness in an indigenous cultural territoriality, an ability also mirrored by Howe in *Shell Shaker*.

Privileging of indigenous "knowledges" is, for us, the assertion of interconnected, overlapping, and/or multivalent insider knowledge systems that are aimed toward a more realistic exploration and portrayal of multifaceted indigenous realities and existences grounded in family, communal, and ancestral existence. The "s" in "knowledges" is essential to this definition because Western scholarship has attempted to confine the indigenous to a unitary, static, backward past, which is ultimately a passé monolith while Western modernity is the here and now of dynamic potential. Thus the "s" entails a vibrant multiplicity of coeval "knowledges" that are dynamic and ever developing in their various expressions of cultural specificity and lived realities and experiences. This indigenous-privileging can be used to provide an independent critique of oppressors of the indigenous peoples and systems of life. It exists independently of Western/ European/ colonial paradigms as a positive assertion and affirmation of complex multiple existences and experiences in art, sciences, scholarship and society. Therefore privileging indigenous "knowledges" is not bound to the role of the oppressed in that Western and modernist binary of postmodernism. It must be recognized first and foremost as a positive, independent, culture-specific approach to literature of indigenous writers and not simply, or ever, as a "post-post-modern" theoretical continuation of Western-privileging in European and American academia.

Walter Mignolo creates and explores the concept of bi-languaging in his work *Local Histories/Global Designs: Coloniality, Subaltern Knowledges and Border Thinking*. In this article, we take his work on coevalness and territoriality a theoretical step further to postulate bi-living as the result of integrating coevalness and the consequent surviving territoriality that is possible in the liminal spaces between and among coeval realities in which the fullness of the indigenous territoriality –often surviving brutal colonial and neo-colonial attacks– can provide the characters an approach to wholeness as indigenous individuals who are also a part of a greater community. Coeval may thus be defined here as a multiplicity of spatial temporalities co-existing and influencing one another, and the lives of individuals and their communities existing in any one of these coeval realities.

The Visitor presents "a world where all life interacts – the unborn, the living, the dead, the ancestors, the past, the present, the good, the bad– in a seeming endless cycle of existence powered by choices" (Emezue 238). The fact that Ce, like Howe in *Shell Shaker*, writes this bi-living into a full coeval reality so that characters may heal from the psychological wounds of multiple colonial and neocolonial assaults introduces a note of hope and continuity for indigenous territoriality with its own implications for space and time conceptions in postcolonial literature.

Bi-living further entails the assumption of indigenous cultural territoriality including a spiritual and coeval acknowledgement and acceptance so that the indigenous standpoint is privileged in this theorization of the Mignolo-inspired concept. Coeval time therefore denotes a rejection of the Western temporal linearity imposed upon the colonized across the world and a privileging of time and space as conceived, perceived, and communicated by indigenous peoples who kept their own sacred, temporal, spatial assumptions and practices despite superficial acceptance and use of the Western linearity. Thus Ce's and Howe's novels echo this conceptual framework of indigenous time and space so that, like Ngugi's Matigari, they reflect the indigenous knowledge that,

The story has no fixed time.
Yesterday, the day before yesterday, last week…
Last year…
Or ten years ago?

Reader/listener: may the action take place in the time of your choice!

And again, it does not demarcate time in terms of seconds

Or minutes

Or hours

Or days.

Reader/listener: may you allocate the duration of any of the actions according to your choice! (ix)

Time, for instance, in *The Visitor* is indigenous, coeval, non-linear and cyclical, so that, as Amanda Grants notes, the three suns of Erin allow an understanding of three coexisting realities in this transcendently conscious indigenous experience (25). The same can be said of the three co-temporal realities set over 200 years apart, spanning the mid 18th century to late 20th century in Howe's *Shell Shaker* which interweaves the role of the peacemaking Billy family in murders involving corrupt Choctaw, Nation of Oklahoma, secular leaders. In both instances, the realities intersect through one character: Deego in *The Visitor*, and Auda Billy in *Shell Shaker*, although the coeval temporalities affect everyone since they seem to run parallel at times and end with a potentially changed future given Deego's and Auda's abilities to anticipate what will change, for the better, the course of their societies' future as well as their own. The collective is just as important as the individual in this reconceptualization of a cyclical collective reality because "from this multi-dimensional perception, man orders his environment and infuses it with positive values like unity, brotherhood, fraternal relationships and (ultimate) spiritual contentment" (Emezue 242).

The anchoring time period of the "past" is one that reveals corruption and chaos in both novels so that the story of Mensa is "seen partly through his narrative consciousness and through the omniscient-narrative point of view to embrace a world of police corruption and decadence in Nigeria, a country drowning in its own degenerate materialism" (Grants 26). A parallel is also set in the decadent and corrupt vision of the Durant, Oklahoma Choctaw Nation which is led by unscrupulous men like Chief Redford McAlester working with the mafia and the Irish Republican Army to exploit the indigenous people and their land, as represented by the Billy family.

The reality for both protagonists —Deego in *The Visitor* and Auda Billy in *Shell Shaker*— is that the corruption in one of the coeval realities is such that affects all of their temporalities, especially their current lives. This comes through invasive dreams/ visions that connect them to different times and realities in which they seem to play an integral part. For instance, Deego is also Mensa, and Erie, and lives their experiences fully as either criminal or amnesiac; Auda is also Anoleta, her great ancestor, who murdered her husband as a debt to her family, and to stop his treacherous behavior which hurt so many indigenous peoples, and to have the potential for a future life in which these same patterns could be stopped. Both Deego and Auda are then able to discern how to change the future and end corruption in their particular nations for the good of the collective, but this knowledge is only gained through delving deeper into the other coeval realities with the help of leaders such as Uzi and Sarah, respectively.

Deego is guided, as the Erie character, to a reintegration of self as a coeval individual who is all three and any single one of the characters at a given moment by the skillful Uzi who claims, "We have launched sixteen million memories to a hundred million different planets since I took over this little place" (58), and warns that "the clash of past and present could cause a malfunction…at the risk of thoughts waving round at the time. It could upset things, and tales of spirits could really unsettle other minds not used to the interpenetrating essence of the universe" (57). In other words, his greater understanding of the many minds limited by modernist linear time informs his decision to tell Erie of a coeval "pluriverse" before he actually experiences it, and the potentially mind-crashing shock that could accompany the experience for one accustomed to linear temporality and spatiality.

Meanwhile Auda and the Billys are guided by Grandmother Porcupine/Divine Sarah who leads various characters through vision about parts of their history. As the embodiment of a trickster character, she makes many claims deemed unbelievable and untrue, just as Uzi's notion of a "pluriverse" is inconceivable to Erie, but which are actually realistic and provide insight into potential solutions to the recurring corruption and attack on the Choctaw community across time. The guides are unconventional for the westernized societies in which the individuals live their other lives but are actually simply embodying the indigenous cosmologies that were alive and intact among some groups of the people despite others' westernization. These cosmologies include orature, conviviality with the sensuous, circular and coeval time, and sacred space. Thus the strange thing about these characters is precisely their indigenous grounding and their full understanding of coeval time in the midst of other coeval realities within the setting of a westernized reality that is limited to a conception of time as linear and space as exclusive.

As Abrams notes in *Spell of the Sensuous*, Europe disparaged indigenous sensorial reality, perception, and connectivity and labeled it inanimate –when it was most alive in the indigenous mind– and "primeval unsettled wilderness" (94) that had to be tamed, civilized, and conquered. All of these European propositions required violence, control, and power and they forced the people to publicly transfer their animism to the alphabet, although many indigenous people also privately retained their connections to the sensuous. Uzi and Sarah are both mediators for the sensuous among those who have lost their connections to indigenous realities, cosmologies, and temporalities.

The coeval reality creates the possibility of using indigenous knowledge systems to understand the various possibilities to change the corrupt present of some of the characters and to move toward a postcolonial reality that is truly post-colonial and not merely corrupt and neocolonial. Thus although African and Native American, these novels share the concept of coevalness which provides a vehicle for recapturing territoriality and the indigenous awareness that have been superficially lost to the interaction and influence of the imperial West.

Here the texts seem to conform to Matigari's claim in Ngugi's work:

This story is imaginary.
The actions are imaginary.
The characters are imaginary.
The country is imaginary... (ix)

and could be applied to other postcolonial imaginaries. Both texts by Chin Ce and LeAnne Howe are strongly grounded in their present Nigerian and U.S. social, political, spiritual and economic conditions, so that the lessons are real and applicable to a concrete reality.

Because "the future, past and present are re-examined closely to show the intermingling of worlds the central character suffers much pain in both physical and spiritual worlds" (Emezue 254). The texts are also imaginary in their resonance with many of the oppressed countries of the world, just as Ngugi's Matigari shares this potential resonance. Deego and Auda engage, therefore, in the quest for identity so that their indigenous territoriality is also at stake in this experience of what Grants calls the cyclical order and Mignolo designates the coeval. The shift is such that both characters shift conceptually "from the structure of a ladder to the structure of a cobweb" (Ogaga 137) in relation to time, and they are able to overcome their helpless current state in the "past" reality which is Mensa's criminality as "a staunch youth of Ironi" in Aja, a corrupt and selfish neocolonial set up, and Anoleta's unproven criminality in the war-tending dispersed Choctaw community of the 1800s, a similarly dysfunctional set up. They move to a world that is all potentiality, namely, Deego's and Auda's world of familial stability so that his family and Auda's Billy clan provide the reality in which they can both change the circumstances of their futures.

The answers to potential futures and the reclamation of their territoriality are provided to Deego by his experience as Erie in Erin, "the idyllic representation of this world of ancestors as custodian of the African heritage" (Grants 27) which is all about healers and teachers who understand the coeval reality of their existence, and to Auda by Sarah and the Billy family who are keenly aware of the cyclical coexistent time that informs the Choctaw's cosmology. Their ability to see the past, future and present as interactive and fluid leads the characters to a potential reintegration of their indigenous selves and knowledge systems into their current reality while remaining informed by the other two temporal spheres. Thus "Chin Ce's entry into the subjective universe of ancestral interactivity offers a unique perspective on contemporaneous and simultaneous levels of existence" (Grants 26). The same is true of Howe's work which exemplifies her premise that "Native stories...seem to pull all the elements together of the storyteller's tribe, meaning the people, the land, and multiple characters and all their manifestations and revelations, and connect these in past, present and future milieus" (Howe 29).

The "daydreams, visions, and nightmares" that Erie experiences are akin to the Coatlicue state described by Gloria Anzaldua in *Borderlands/ La Frontera* and lead to an integration of the coeval self. These intersecting milieus allow for a changed future that can be different from the Aja of Mensa's reality and lead to a more hopeful Nigerian future of community-centered self-governance which "could free so many, open some blind corners, and push the whole of humankind further ahead than the darkness into which it has degenerated" (Ce 190). It could further move Anoleta's and Auda's initial experience of the Choctaw nation to the unification of the Choctaw people evident in their coming together for the communal burial, on sacred ground, of Red Shoes with all his money and belongings so that his Spirit, content with material goods, may remain with them and cease to plague the Choctaw with corruption, greed, and war. Thus the two characters conceive of new ways to lead their lives, their communities, and their nations to a more indigenous paradigm of living which honors the need for community, taking care of each other, and territoriality in which to exercise their indigenous practices.

The Visitor and *Shell Shaker* while clearly privileging indigenous knowledge systems must be seen as an opportunity taken by the writers for "constructing new loci of enunciation as well as for reflecting that academic 'knowledge and understanding' should be complemented with 'learning from' those who are living and thinking from colonial and postcolonial legacies" (Mignolo 5). In other words, these texts privilege alternative centers of enunciation for "indigenous use," as Frederick Cooper argues in *Colonialism in Question: Theory Knowledge, History*. Both works are part of the literature engagee produced by "writers of the continent [who] are often classified as engaged writers, as instruments of change whose job is to expose, in one way or another, the evils of society" (Ogaga 138). Although Ce and Howe hail from different continents, their aims align, and the comparison of their work yields a better understanding of the indigenous cosmologies they represent and the potential for regeneration under the guidance of the ancestors, the various houses of communal memory, and the experience of coevalness.

Just as the narrative arc of Ce centers on the growth and development of a character who experiences three coeval existences, so Howe provides a similar narrative arc for Auda Billy with similar presumptions about indigenous cosmologies, temporalities, and spatiality, namely territoriality. Both novels plunge "into the abode of the ancestors to reveal the positive attributes of a complementary beingness" (Emezue 258). Once the coeval is acknowledged and utilized as a valuable indigenous tool in these narratives, the central characters, along with their co-characters, can create a new reality for themselves that is the product of the knowledge they have gained from interacting in these three realms of existence, and they posit an "unbreakable thread and posit a statement on the continuation of individual responsibility over and above mere existential needs" (Grants 25).

The Visitor and *Shell Shaker* posit the reclamation of their territoriality that had been erased, at least according to European sources, by the experience of colonialism. It is a territoriality that will allow the collective to heal and to continue the indigenous privileging that is life giving, not the Western *Osano* (bloodsucker) practices of Aja. The coevalness of Ce's *The Visitor* is necessarily the product of an African, specifically Nigerian, indigenous bi-living because his text acts out the living contact between the various coeval realities –both temporal and spatial– and the important knowledge that can be gained in the interstitial spaces of contact, influence, and redefinition. Here the novelist "moves seamlessly between philosophical reflection and the description of intimate details of everyday life" (Ogaga 139) and grants the reader an insight into the potentiality of coevalness for regeneration of a "socio-economic emancipation which the political leaders are unable to provide for the masses of the continent" (138) because they function as comprador petit-bourgeoisie, no longer caring for the masses but interested only in imperial links –economic and social– for self-benefit. In Anibal Quijano's terms, it is here, in this coeval temporal reality, that the tree of knowledge meets the tree of life, and it is here that the survival of African cultural territorialities, per Mignolo's terminology in *The Darker Side of the Renaissance*, can be both theorized and realized.

As clearly shown, this finding is also applicable to Howe's novel, for it is the product of a Native American, specifically Choctaw, indigenous bi-living experience. Howe's *Shell Shaker* performs the interstitial living of the Choctaw and the liminality that allows for growth from generation to interacting cyclical generation. Chin Ce and LeAnne Howe also create for their characters a development that takes place also across coeval realities and spaces which render the individual not only responsible for the collective but also a potential harbinger of hope and life for a corrupt society. As evidenced by these texts Native American Choctaw cosmology, much like that of the African, is informed by coeval realities and shapes the philosophy of values in art and life in society (Emezue 260).

Ngugi's *Matigari*, another seminal text of African postcolonial literature, provides an intrusive grounding of these coeval and territorial tenets laid out in Ce's and Howe's novels so that Aja and Durant are, in essence, comparable to the world that meets Ngugi's Matigari when he emerges from the forest: corruption rules and violence is the norm. Matigari is, like the wise ones in Erin, and Sarah's and Auda's ancestors are able to envision a better world, a new revolutionary outlook, free of the neocolonial comprador petite bourgeois who, for personal gain, sell out indigenous peoples to the West. Ngugi's Matigari, like Ce's Deego and Howe's Auda, is poised to bring out the best in the masses so that they can work together toward an ideological revolution instead of simply parroting without actual change, namely, the post-independence sham. Thus Matigari can, along with the characters of Ce's and Howe's novels, chant in the workers' voices, the voices of the peasants, the voices of the students and of other patriots of all the different nationalities of the land, singing in harmony:

> Victory shall be ours!
> Victory shall be ours!
> Victory shall be ours!
> Victory shall be ours! (175)

Ultimately Ce's *The Visitor* and Howe's *Shell Shaker* create a parallel vision of an indigenous society that engages and heals itself in bi-living. By doing so, these texts open spaces for a coeval ack-nowledgement of ancestors, past lives, openness to understanding multiple indigenous realities and co-existences, and radical activism for the collective good.

Chapter 4

The Ancestral Diaspora

The Middle Passage and Lost Ancestors

THE biblical prophet Ezekiel's infamous vision of a *valley of dry ancestral bones* that is brought to life then rebuilt as a new living people has often been appropriated by black intellectuals and artists as both a signifier for the historical dispersal of peoples of the African Diaspora and as a redemptive narrative that suggests that diasporic body can be re-born through the restoration of the dead. More importantly, the commemoration of the ancestor figure anchors the diasporic subject to their own uncertain present by enabling them to redeem the past. Furthermore, these stories about the re-animation of flesh and bone signify the multiple ways that communities of blacks across the globe envision the afterlife of oppression. This search and cultural reclamation of an African origin and/or roots is often tied to the solemn remembrance of the *Ancestor*. Thus the demand for the humane treatment of the *ancestral dead* is viewed as having both social and psychic consequences for the generations that follow (Rushdy 43).

For many Black artists throughout the Diaspora, the aesthetic recovery of African origins often serves as a way to bridge those ruptures that exist between the uncertain present and the elusive past. As the renowned African American playwright August Wilson articulates in *The Ground on which I Stand*, "all of art is a search for a way of being" (46). For Wilson, the stage serves as symbolic space of cultural rebirth—it is a way of being, which he views as being invested with the strength of his African ancestors (19-20). Consequently, many of his plays highlight the need for modern black subjects not only to reclaim their cultural and spiritual ties to Africa, but also to craft new histories and/or mythologies that produce progressive narratives of diasporic cross-cultural connections framed within a network of genealogical affiliation. As Wilson articulates himself, "the message of America is to leave your Africanness out the door. My message is claim what is yours" (Freedman "Voice").

This powerful declaration, "claim what is yours," is a call for both a cultural and spiritual renewal bound to reclamation of the ancestral dead, which is a theme that resonates throughout many of Wilson's plays. Like many other black artists within the Diaspora, Wilson chooses to return to tragic waters of Middle Passage in order to explore its theoretical and aesthetic resonances as an imagined point of interconnection for African descendants dispersed throughout the New World. Furthermore, he sees the African American aesthetic tradition as being embodied by a spirit of triumph which spans from Africans' journey from the hull of the ship to their journey as a self-respecting people (Wilson *Ground* 36-38). Wilson affirms Caribbean theorist Édouard Glissant's dictum that terror of the unknown born on the tragic waters of the passage inadvertently became an epistemology of diasporic ontology which also became a "freeing knowledge of Relation within the whole" (Glissant 9). In other words, the Atlantic Ocean serves as a rhizomatic space of diasporic connection, joined by intertwined histories and cosmogonies—which ultimately embodies a *vast beginning* (6) for black subjects in both continental Africa and the Diaspora. Thus Wilson invokes the image of the oceanic grave of the Atlantic as a way to reformulate originary narratives which tie diasporic subjects to their African past. Wilson seeks to reclaim those African ancestors, whom writers like Toni Morrison describe as the "millions of people disappeared without a trace [to] never arrive safely on shore" (Furman 80), by exploring the aquatic genealogies which bridge the African American experience to the African ancestral past in his twentieth-century cycle plays, *Joe Turner's Come and Gone* (1984), and *Gem of the Ocean* (2002). At the center of each of these plays is a celebration of the incredible spirituality of African people who honor their ancestors (Dezell 255). Moreover, Wilson's historical reclamation of the ancestor figure highlights the ways in which progress is often read as a form of redress for both the living and the dead within the black Diaspora. More importantly, he suggests that the "ghostly aspects of social life" (Gordon 197) which haunt the black Diaspora creates an intersubjectivity—a superimposition of the past upon the present—of flesh upon flesh that can only be resolved through the invocation of the ancestral past. Indeed, for Wilson, the sacred remembrance of the "Ancestor" signifies a semi transformation for the living—a reclamation of African Ancestors who secure the collective diasporic body in place within a narrative of redemption and/or belonging.

Re-Connecting the Bones: Joe Turner's Come and Gone

The Ghanaian poet Kwadwo Opuku-Agyemang describes the history of transatlantic slavery as a "living wound under a patchwork of scars" (3) which marks the collective body of descendants in both the Diaspora and continental Africa. The poet suggests that the enduring pain of slavery is embodied by the loss of those ancestors who were cut out of Africa's womb and carried away on a tragic voyage "through burning oceans" (3). Opuku-Agyemang's account of the interconnected traumas enacted by the Middle Passage on both sides of the Atlantic serves as a generational story "strewn across several times zones and territories" (Hanchard 49), which is deployed as a way of making meaning of the loss and ruptures that characterize the relationship between the Diaspora and Africa. Consequently, Opuku-Agyemang situates African captives' journey across "burning oceans" within a narrative of genealogical and diasporic affiliation. So too, African American dramatist, August Wilson, returns to the ocean to excavate and/or reconstitute an origin story for the Diaspora, infusing such traditional sites of horror as the Middle Passage with symbolic power. Such a writer as critic Sandra G. Shannon asserts:

> sees himself as a 'conduit of antecedents,' giving voice to millions of African ancestors and their descendants —from slaves tossed overboard during the Middle Passage to his grandmother, who reportedly walked from North Carolina to Pittsburgh during the post-Reconstruction exodus of blacks from the south (6).

This reclamation of ties of kinship which bind the living to the dead of the Middle Passage is a particular facet of much of Wilson's work, especially resonant in his plays *Joe Turner's Come and Gone* (1988) and *Gem of the Ocean* (2002). Both plays are part of a ten-play cycle—used to chronicle the black experience over a span of century, by having each play set in a different decade. His play *Joe Turner's Come and Gone* (abbreviated *JTCAG*) is set in a Pittsburgh boardinghouse in 1911 and uses a sort of "Grand Hotel" strategy to take in a number of characters who are searching for a racial and spiritual identity (Powers 3). Wilson focuses on the plight of African American migrants who journey from the south looking for brighter prospects and opportunities in the industrial north. These characters are described as the sons and daughters of newly freed Africans—cut off from memory, and who have now forgotten the names of the gods (*JTCAG* Prologue).

Most of these characters are treated as "foreigners in a strange land" (Prologue); finding no solace, they wander aimlessly and slowly lose those cultural ties which bind them to both their slave past and African heritage. These are also people who have not reconciled the traumas of the slave past that reach into the present. For example, the central character of the play, Harold Loomis, is a figure that is plagued and haunted by the harrowing memories of his past. As Wilson writes, "he is a man driven not by the hellhounds that seemingly bay at this heels but a search for a world that speaks to something about himself" (3-14). What's more, Loomis personifies those millions of slaves who were freed after the Civil War, were besieged by confusion and doubt about the future, which is inherently informed by a break from their ancestral past (Powers 9). Ultimately, Loomis must counter this sense of disconnection and loss by marking a place for himself within the long line of African ancestors who inhabit the bottom of the ocean.

In contrast to Loomis, who is deeply ambivalent about his spiritual and ancestral connections to the slave past, most of the other characters in the play maintain a "distinctive spirituality that [..] has its roots in Africa" (Murphy 1). August Wilson highlights this "interdependence between the community and spirit" (2) in a scene where the inhabitants of the boarding house participate in the Juba. In a mood of festiveness, the inhabitants collectively decide to "Juba down!" (*JTCAG* 51) after their Sunday dinner. The stage directions read:

The Juba is reminiscent of the Ring Shouts of the African slaves. It is a call and response dance. [...] It should be as African as possible, with the performers working themselves up into near frenzy. The words can be improvised, but should include some mention of the Holy Ghost (52).

The Juba is a syncretic blend of African American and African styles of ritual performance. It is the most popular and most enduring of all the slave clapping songs which, like the traditional African American ring shout, incorporate a synthesis of African styles of ancestor invocation.1 Wilson suggests that the cultural ruptures created on the Middle Passage did not completely obliterate the black Diaspora's link to Africa as embodied by the characters' ritual performance of the Juba. As Harry Elam writes: "Wilson implicitly and explicitly connects the Juba moment in *Joe Turner* to such African traditions of spiritual and social empowerment by granting the actors the license to improvise" (204). In other words, the Juba scene simultaneously serves as both a dramatic representation and an authentic invocation of the ancestor figure in that the actors must fuse art and spiritual practice.

The protagonist Loomis eventually interrupts this moment of cheerfulness amongst the inhabitants of the boarding house as he collapses on the floor haunted by a vision of bones rising up and walking across the water. Loomis declares:

They just walking across the water [...] and then they sunk down [...] All at one time! They just all fell into the water at one time [...] When they sink down they made a big splash and this here wave come up... [...] It washed them out of the water and up on the land. Only...only [...] They got flesh on them! Just like you and me! [...] They ain't moved or nothing. They just laying there. [...] I'm laying there...waiting [...] I got to stand up. I can't

71

lay here no more. All the breath coming into my body and I got to stand up […] The ground's starting to shake. There's a great shaking. The world's busting half in two. The sky's splitting open. I got to stand up […] Got to stand up […] I got to stand up. Get up on the road. […] My legs won't stand up! My legs won't stand up! (*JCTAG* 54-55)

Loomis's apocalyptic vision of bones sinking and then rising out of the water–subsequently re-fleshed and then washed onto the land–recalls the biblical connotations of the prophet Ezekiel's vision of a valley of bones coming to life in the desert in order to redeem the dispersed Israelites. It also bears some resemblance to the Christian story of Jesus's resurrection. However, it is clear that this is an alternative reading of redemption, which privileges the symbolic reintegration of the ancestral dead within a new and living community of disenfranchised blacks who are also waiting to *breathe again* in the tumultuous wake of loss and devastation embedded in the era of American post-Reconstruction. The vision also serves as a symbolic enactment of Loomis's re-birth. For example, the "shaking ground" replicates the violent motions of a contracting womb, whereas the bones coming out of the water enacts the process of physical birth. Moreover, Loomis's own physical inability to stand also signals his status as an infant who is newly "re-born" and who must learn to walk again as a new man. Christopher Bigsby asserts:

In Joe Turner's Come and Gone, the self-imposed function of one character is to bring people back together,

72

to reunite those who have been broken apart. Although each individual has to heal himself or herself, that process involves the recognition of a community in the present and over time. In particular, they [have] to recognize that they [are] African people, despite the passage of time. That connection becomes stronger the further Wilson moves back in time. (12)

Consequently, Loomis's "re-birth" serves as a larger symbol of the African American community's reclamation of their African past. As Harry Elam Jr. suggests, "Loomis's frightening, yet mystical 'rememory' of 'bones walking on top of the water' captures the dichotomy of those perilous journeys aboard slave ships that marked both death and new life, that ensured the profound disconnection from, as well as the endurance of the spirit of Africa, that initiated the complex gestation and difficult birth of African Americans" (3). The birth of the Diaspora begins with this novel articulation of famlial and kinship ties as descendants' new and emergent sense of collective identity is informed by their bond to the dead. So too, the commemoration of those African ancestors tragically lost to the abyss of history helps to forge new and long-lasting forms of kinship, which signify the symbolic reconstitution of a new collective body joined by the experiences of loss.

Wilson also suggests that the cultural ruptures brought on by the tragedies of the transatlantic slavery can be transcended through an alternative and metaphysical understanding of the Middle Passage, which helps to revitalize descendants' understanding of their ties to their ancestral past. For example, as the play ends, the central character Loomis declares "I'm standing now!" (93). Consequently, as Loomis utters these last words, the lights eventually fade out, and the stage directions read: "[…] fully resurrected, cleansed and given breath, free from any encumbrance other than the workings of his own heart […] [Loomis] is free to soar above the environs that weighed and pushed his spirit into terrifying contractions" (94). Loomis's personal affirmation of both his corporeal and spiritual power is firmly aligned with a new and revitalized sense of his membership within the world of the *bones people*. Significantly, Wilson asks his audience to reconsider the symbolic connotations of such icons of historical wreckage, as embodied by the Middle Passage, by reconstructing it as a sacred space of interconnection which links both the ancestral dead to their descendants. As August Wilson declares: "this is who you are. You are these bones. You are the sons and daughters of these people" (Powers 9). Consequently, Loomis's personal redemption is brought on by his reclamation of himself as member of a re-constituted collective body that is born of both flesh and spirit.

A Scattered Road Home: Gem of the Ocean

August Wilson invokes a city of bones submerged deep within the ocean in his play *Gem of the Ocean* (2002), which "reunites or re-members the collective black body, [and] those lost old bones, [by turning] them into a unified and communal site" (Elam 236). *Gem of the Ocean* is the first portion of his decade-by-decade ten play cycle that is set in 1904. Just as in Wilson's *Joe*

Turner's Come and Gone, Gem of the Ocean is set in the steel-mill towns of turn-of-the-century Pittsburgh, and it also recounts the story of troubled male character named Citizen Barlow who like Harold Loomis is searching for redemption. Citizen Barlow seeks help from Aunt Esther—a central character in the play who serves more as a mythical figure than a real character in that she exists in the symbolic space between the world of the spirit and the flesh (Elam 234-35). Aunt Esther also bears symbolic resemblance to *Mami Wata* (See Fig. 1), an African water divinity from the oral tradition of Ghana and Nigeria who was added to the ancient pantheon of African water deities soon after Africans made their first encounter with Europeans in the fifteenth century (Drewal 193). Many believe that she crossed the water with her subjects during the Middle Passage. For example Aunt Esther States:

I done see all the adventure I want to see. I been across the water. I seen both sides of it. I know about the water [...] I came across that ocean, Mr. Citizen. I cried. I had lost everything. Everything I had known in this life I lost that. I cried a ocean of tears. Everything I had known in this life was gone (*Gem* 52-53).

Aunt Esther is a mythic figure who claims to have seen "both sides" of the ocean. Like Mami Wata, who is also known as the mother of the water, she is a healer who bears the responsibility of reconnecting diasporic subjects to their African past. In this way, as Carl Pedersen contends, "the Middle Passage emerges as more of a bridge than a breach, a space-in-between where memory entails reconstructing the horrors of the voyage and retracing the journey of Africans to the Americas" (43). This symbolic transformation and/or re-articulation of the horrors of the voyage can be described as what Joseph Roach defines as cultural surrogation. Roach suggests that a culture often reproduces and recreates itself through surrogation–a process that involves survivors attempts to fit satisfactory alternates into the cavities created by loss through death or other forms of departure (2). Thus the dead emerge as *satisfactory surrogates* for those lost and broken histories, cosmogonies, and ties of kinship, which the survivors of the passage tragically left behind. In essence, these figures, especially embodied by the character Aunt Esther, become the *gods of the Middle Passage* (Dayan 726), a term which denotes "how [African] histories are made anew" through the renaming of the dead."2 These *gods* emerge from physical death, from the holds of the slaveship, and are re-created through the collective conscious of the Diaspora. As Joan Dayan contends:

These gods are utterly corporeal, and once reborn in worship, once returned from under the waters, they bear the traits, the bruises and battering of bodies named and claimed. Brathwaite knows that resistance lies in renaming the gods, reclaiming the bodies, [and] repeating but also redefining history. (726)

Dayan suggests that the emergent Diasporic consciousness which was born on the passage is shaped not only by the captives' retentions of traditional African culture but also by the new modes of sociality which link the dead and the living. Consequently, Aunt Esther's mythic position between both the Old and New World allows for a reconstructed genealogy that binds disparate subjects into a *living community* transformed by their reclamation of the ancestral dead of the Middle Passage.

Wilson also invokes many of Orlando Patterson's theories on slavery and social death within his play. For example, Patterson contends that the domination of the slave results in a negation of his existence which constitutes a form of social death (38). Drawing on Hegel's theory of the Master/Slave dialectic, Paterson also notes: "for the slave, freedom begins with the consciousness that real life comes with the negation of his social death", in other words, "the reclamation of that life must therefore be the negation of this negation" (97-98). It might be suggested that Wilson's aesthetic return to the violent waters of the Middle Passage serves as a form of historical reclamation designed to "negate the negation" of those lost ancestral bodies by simultaneously recognizing the devastation and cultural links that emerge on the passage, which subsequently impact the living and the dead. Indeed, the protagonist Citizen Barlow's own redemption is enacted through his sacred reclamation of the ancestral dead of the Middle Passage. As with the character Harold Loomis in *Joe Turner's Come and Gone*, the bones of the ancestor serve as a spiritual compass designed to lead the protagonist back home.

Citizen Barlow, plagued by guilt for inadvertently causing the death of a coworker, shows up on Aunt Esther's doorstep seeking absolution for his deeds. Towards the end of scene two in Act One Citizen Barlow unburdens his soul to Aunt Esther and declares: "I was gonna go to another city but then before I had a chance I killed a man. I don't know, Miss Tyler. I feel like I got a hole inside me. People say you can help me. I don't want to go to hell" (Gem 23). Citizen Barlow believes that Aunt Esther can cleanse him of the guilt he feels for causing Garret Brown's death. Garret Brown is a character who chooses to drown in a river rather than falsely admit to stealing a bucket of nails actually stolen by Citizen. As Aunt Esther observes, "that was the only way he [Garret] had to say he was innocent [...] He was willing to die to say that" (21). Aunt Esther reads Garret's suicide as a form of redemption, thus his death by water is also an active form of resistance which reverses loss into spiritual transcendence. Consequently, Aunt Esther decides that Citizen must also return to the water, and provides him with a map that will enable him to journey to the *City of Bones*. Described as "only a half mile by half mile", the city of bones is mythic underwater world inhabited by the victims of the Middle Passage; it is a place where, as Aunt Esther declares, "all the buildings and everything is made up of bones. The trees are made of bones. All the palaces are glittering with the light of the sun. [And] the streets look like silver" (66). Harry Elam asserts:

> The City of Bones is the mystical, spiritual city below the surface of the water where lost black souls have come to rest. It is built from the bones of those who perished on the perilous journey across the ocean that was the Middle Passage [...] For Citizen Barlow, traveling to the City of Bones equally means reconnecting with his past.

Functioning ritualistically, his journey removes his earlier sins and psychological burdens. (Elam 235, 242)

Thus the watery grave of the Middle Passage is transformed—serving now as a sort of ritual space of cultural initiation—for those dispersed subjects seeking historical redemption. Citizen Barlow goes to the *City of Bones* not only to get his soul cleansed but also to mend the temporal breach between the ancestral past and the immediate present as he is forced to re-experience the traumas of the Middle Passage himself through an induced vision. In Wilson's stage directions for the scene,

They symbolically brand and symbolically whip Citizen, then throw him into the hull of the boat. The hatch slams shut. Citizen finds himself alone. [...] Citizen begins to sing an African lullaby to himself, a song his mother taught him. Then he is thirsty [...] Black Mary begins to sing 'Twelve Gates to the City.' Hearing the song, Citizen slowly unfolds from his fetal position. All is calm and peaceful. He stands up and looks to see the most beautiful sight he has ever seen. He has arrived at the City of Bones. He is awed by its beauty. (Wilson *Gem* 67-68)

Citizen's metaphysical and physical journey on the slave ship "Gem of the Ocean" is not tied to any one specific historical narrative about the Middle Passage. It is clear that, for Wilson, history becomes secondary to the imagination, which is often the dominant force at work in such historical recreations of the past (Shannon 4). Wilson is far more invested in crafting a new mythology of the Middle Passage embodied by the sacred commemoration of the 'Ancestor.' Wilson suggests that "it's important for bodies to be exhumed [because] in doing so you return dignity to the dead" (Philip 202). Like many other Black artists throughout the Diaspora, Wilson also "returns dignity to dead" by drawing a relationship between the Middle Passage and Africa, which also serves as a form of redemption for the living—who are now sanctified by those ancestral bones lying deep within the murky abyss of the Middle Passage.

Return and Recuperation

The history of the Middle Passages "continues to haunt us because", as Ian Baucom contends, "it points to the impossibility of historical ending in that the time of dying does not sunder itself from the time of living but fills life with its painful weight" (332). It might be suggested that the desire to re-imagine and/or revise the narrative which surrounds the Middle Passage highlights the ways in which black subjects often return to the traumas of the past as a way to re-assert their cultural ties to Africa. The African American dramatist August Wilson also suggests that there is an inherent value to be found in the return to such a profound site of past horrors as embodied by the Middle Passage. Offering more than just a way to redefine cultural identities, the figuration of such tragic sites of memory as the Middle Passage within the complex and myriad network of diasporic "generational stories" might help us subvert those narratives which read historical loss as historical defeat. More importantly, as historian Vincent Brown suggests, "in the struggle to shape the future the dead do not necessarily have the last word, but they always have a voice."3 Thus the attempt to recover both a genealogical and ancestral narrative tied to such a massive space of loss serves as much more than epistemic and/or aesthetic exercise—it signifies the courage to straddle two cultural spaces, to tie the precarious present to an ancestral African past, and to find a way to make a home in those two worlds.

Chapter 5

Modernity and African Identity

SM Jha

WHEN we talk of identity crisis in African writing it is a kind that is both individual and territorial in character and does have strong social, political, religious or cultural implications within the continent. We recognize that a century of colonial governance saw African countries losing much of their traditional and cultural identities to artificial nation state and ideological formations becoming "artifices and colonies of Europe existing for economic administrative purposes of Imperialism with no respect for cultural or filial bonds of their own people" (Ce 38). The violence inscribed upon the continent by the colonizing power witnessed traumatic physical and psychological conditions that affected generations of African peoples and cultures. For the first generation of modern African writers led by Senghor, Achebe, etc., it was a daunting task to seek to restore belief in the lost and maligned traditions of Africa via literature. These efforts coalesced in the focus of African literature to deal with the qualities of human nature through intense examination of the forces of history upon valid personal and national aspirations. Its politics is concerned with universal communication across racial and cultural boundaries as a means of fostering respect for the people. Today this Pan-African restoration of identity has gained in relevance beyond the borders of the continent and beyond the anthropological, sociological, and political concerns of post-colonial Africa.

Chinua Achebe emerged on the literary scene of Nigeria at a time when the conflict between his countrymen and the English rulers of his land had reached its highest point of tension. Writing at a time when Africans were not only opposing European rule through political action, but were also beginning to question with increasing vigor and clarity the cultural assumption used to justify their rule, Achebe through his novels *Things Fall Apart* (1958), *No Longer at Ease* (1960) and *Arrow of God* (1964) sought to show that the subjection of Africa by alien races had brought disaster upon the African psyche. These writings present a kaleidoscopic vision of the African society, exhibiting a concern for that rich native culture whose extirpation is threatened by imported Western patterns of life. Achebe could appreciate the religious concomitants of the other cultures and simultaneously use the same appreciation to defend his own. His immense stylistic vigor charged with a powerful realism and often satirical candor is not seduced by the new nationalism but it challenges the corruption of thought and action in the emergent Africa and revives the moral values of society. Achebe does have a cultivated habit of thinking over problems, and it is quite in the fitness of things that he wrote *A Man of the People* (1966) on this particular and precise theme, that is, the bleak prospects of a country that is being governed by outsiders. The crisis engendered by this infamous legacy continues to be of paramount interest to African writers.

Achebe's fourth novel focuses on the tribulations of a Nigerian teacher who joins a political group working to remove a corrupt bureaucrat from office thereby highlighting the widespread graft and abuse of power by Nigerian leaders following its independence from Britain. It was extremely unfortunate that soon after independence Nigeria got plunged into a state of civil war; democracy was stifled and smothered; military coups took place bringing in their wake repressive forms of dictatorship with the result that the social, political, religious and cultural identity of Nigeria was once again threatened and endangered. *A Man of the People* is a sharp comment on the corruption and personality cult in African states modeled on Nigeria. Its publication on the 24th of January, 1966, a few days after the military coup that overthrew the corrupt government and outlawed all political parties till further notice, created a sensation not only in the political circles but also among critics of modern African writing.

There have been other Nigerian efforts to offer a long ranging view of the modern nation-state in later novels like Soyinka's *The Interpreters* (1984) and Ce's *Trilogy* (2008). However, the difference that separates these writers from Achebe consists in the fact that while the former inject much subtlety and experimentation in their works, Achebe is forthright, direct and bristling in approach. Although an element of propaganda is inevitable in any of these writings—and this is also evident of Indian fiction in English as B. Bhattacharya's

So Many Hungers, Khushwant Singh's *Train to Pakistan* and Raj Anand's *Untouchable* reveal– nevertheless the greatness of a creative writer lies in transforming overt or covert propaganda into acceptable literary creation and Achebe achieves this in great measure. Achebe goes straight way into the root of the basic crisis that cripples the progress, prosperity and moral transcendence of his country in particular and the whole of Africa in general. His novels, like few other African novels which followed, clearly expose colonialism and racism as a political contrivance antithetical to black identity, a subjection that reduces man to a beast of burden.

Crisis of Modern Identity: A Man of the People

While Achebe received much critical acclaim for this novel, many looked upon the artist as a far-sighted political emissary while others sought to interpret his achievement as an exercise in prophecy. *A Man of the People* was debated upon either as an 'African parable' or as a 'Nigerian prophecy', a pointer to the social, political and cultural debasement that Nigeria was to undergo in the years to come. It is, in fact, Achebe's 'timely utterance', perhaps his last resolve before the publication of *Anthills of the Savannah*, two decades later, to warn his fellow countrymen that all is not well with the modern nation state and her new fangled demagogues of western democracy.

With Achebe's artistic premonition in *A Man of the People* inviting adulations to himself as 'seer' or 'prophet' for the military coup, which not only concludes the novel but, in a way, pre-determines

Nigeria's political fate as well, Bernth Lindfors makes an effort to examine this parable-prophecy paradigm in detail, and concludes that *A Man of the People* was "a devastating satire in which Achebe heaped scorn on independent Africa" (149). Lindfors further notes:

I believe Achebe ended the novel with a military coup in order to enlarge the picture to include Nigeria's neighbors, many of which have experienced coups. By universalizing the story in this way Achebe could suggest to his countrymen that what had happened in other unstable independent African countries might easily have happened in Nigeria too. The coup was meant as an African parable, not a Nigerian prophecy. (149)

We see Ngugi wa Thiong'o proposing to move away from this controversy to explore the ethical responsibility which may have prompted Achebe to write the novel:

What Achebe has done in *A Man of the People* is to make it impossible or inexcusable for other African writers to do other than address themselves directly to their audiences in Africa not in a comforting spirit – and tell them that such problems are their concern. The teacher no longer stands apart to contemplate. He has moved with a whip among the pupils, flagellating himself as well as them. He is now the true man of the people. (281-82)

Ngugi's observation may have ascribed a function to Achebe's art and united the art with the artist but

Gareth Griffith tries to explore the unbounded force of Achebe's linguistic style which gives his novels that ironic shift from the traditional to the modern, from clarity to ambiguity, and from identity to depersonalization. He argues that as a writer seeking to define the interaction of two cultures Achebe needs more than a single linguistic standard by which to define the moral dilemma of his characters and thereby acknowledges Achebe's efforts. In *A Man of the People* he notices a major technical innovation, since it is the first of the novels to omit the direct intervention of the narrator, placing the onus on the reader to decipher the grammar of values not only through the central character or single rhetoric procedure but also through the variety which the writer offers. To establish the veracity of his observation Griffith presents contradictory views of two eminent critics. While Bernth Lindfors on one hand views that Odili Samalu is a man whose clear vision provides an undistorted view of a warped society, Arthur Ravenscraft on the other hand observes that

Odili is both serious accuser and comically self accused in the rotten society of *A Man of the People*. It isn't simply a matter of contrast between Odili's word and his performance, but a question of how the words themselves reveal a shallow personality: the smirking, familiar 'I know- what I'm- talking- about' tone of so many T.V. Commentators. (77)

Thus Achebe's search for enduring human qualities in a time of crisis takes ironic manifestations in *A Man of*

The People wherein he portrays two well-rounded characters immersed in their own rationale of success and achievement. Although told from the first-person narrative the novelist gives a detached treatment to the course of events. The potential of the novel intensifies through that essential love-hate relationship between the two central characters which binds and unbinds them. The phase of association and alienation are worked out with patience and the novel proceeds with cultivated realism. It is, at the same time, a subtle pointer to the inadequate perception of the British administration regarding the tribal and territorial framework of that African society.

The colonizers did well to consolidate the multitudinous tribes of Nigeria under one territorial head in a democratic manner. But they failed to contend the heat and despondency that segregated them earlier. This tribal sensitiveness is a characteristic feature of all his novels, the relevance being greater in the urban, educated setting in *No Longer at Ease* and *A Man of the People*. In the latter it rises to demonic heights exploiting and extorting an exorbitant price under the pretext of tribal allegiance. The society fails to enact any stringent measures against individuals asserting their individuality against community will and so the social firmament depends upon, or takes shape in, individual loyalties. The society, in its turn, stands as a mute spectator nodding, not in apprehension as in *Things Fall Apart* but, ironically, in appreciation. The confusion and loss of identity which accompanied the social changes have lulled the African spirit into deep slumber where no ethic, no specific cultural value, but its silhouette, appears. In fact, the very meaning of these values has been either subverted or altered in the 'eat and let others eat' regime.

The crisis in *A Man of the People* begins with the acceptance of Chief the Honorable M.N. Nanga, M.P. as the most approachable politician in the country and one who, to his village folks, was a man of the people. This general opinion is presented by the narrator, Odili Samalu, a school teacher at the Anata Grammar School and a former student of Chief Nanga. Nanga is the politician in power: the Minister of culture in a duly elected, democratic form of government. He is one of those political survivalists in the post-independence era whose professional morality rests on maneuvering for themselves seats in the cabinet. Nanga's adaptability to the political scene is commendable. Sensing an empty ministerial seat, he yaps and snarls for hours to condemn the Minister of Finance who has Ph.D. in Public Finance as against his own Standard Six qualification. On the other hand, his public appearances are solemnized through an infectious smile and an irresistible personality. The electorate is yet to imbibe the concept of democracy in its full force and Achebe imparts an ironic twist to their dilemma:

They were not only ignorant but cynical. Tell them that this man has used his position to enrich himself and they would ask you − as my father did − if you thought that a sensible man would spit out the juicy morsel that good fortune placed in his mouth. (2)

In their ignorance they fail to realize that in a democratic set-up 'the juicy morsel' is often a compounding of the bare necessities of the less privileged ones, which is more often the rural uneducated voters. Their cynicism results from their fatalistic approach towards life; what matters now is an appropriation of wealth. Their applause of the hackneyed phrase—national cake—gives us a further insight into their mental frame work. Despite a specific boundary, their minds are yet to be detribalized in favor of their country. M.Ps like Nanga and Koko exploit this untutored naivety.

Nanga's distinction further lies in his kaleidoscopic personality. He travels in a Cadillac, wears damask and gold chains. His participation and squandering of money is a winsome effort which the rural society cannot resist. Duped by this exhibition of cordiality, they fail to fathom what is going behind the scene. To them Nanga is indeed a tribal chief returning home. He has a jovial word for everyone, and by characterizing his visit as a 'family reunion—pure and simple' he, in a way, reduces the whole of Anata to his allegiance. He is a keen observer of human responses and so is able to placate their itch for recognition by a friendly nod here and an expression of feigned respect there.

As for the narrator, he is a skeptical idealist thoroughly disillusioned with the political affairs of the country. He is a witness to the shameful process of eliminating the finance minister and his colleagues for their judicious plan to deal with the dangerous financial crisis through cutting down the price paid to coffee planters as subsidy. The declamation of the miscreant gang, as they were termed later, and which had as its member 'all university people and highly professional men', was polarized by power-craving politicians whose individual interests were above the national interest. By rejecting the proposal of the finance minister, they had led the country into the trap of inflation. A fastidious observer, Odili, preserves a cutting of the editorial publication that had denounced the miscreant gang:

Let us now and for all times extract from our body political as a dentist extracts a stinking tooth all those decadent stooges versed in text book economics and aping the white man's mannerisms and way of speaking...an African from his rich and ancient culture and puts him above his people. (4)

This political propaganda is indeed instrumental in whipping up emotions by suggesting a cultural revival to an unsuspecting electorate. By enumerating time and again the troubles of being a minister, Nanga, tries to drill into the mind of the crowd the immensity of his work, engaging their sympathies for the coming elections:

To God who made me, Minister de sweet for eye but too much katakata de for inside.' 'It is left to Josiah to decipher his real intentions and contradict him, though light heartedly: 'Me one,' he said, 'I no kuku mind the katakata wey de for inside. Make you put Minister money for my hand and all the wahala on top. I no mind at all. (16)

Thus, in the very first chapter, Achebe establishes certain facts about Nanga. However, it is just the tip of the iceberg which the narrator will gradually explore and, in the process, reveal himself as the second, but equally fallacious, alternative. Disenchanted by the political affairs of his country Odili alienates himself from politics and takes up a 'teaching job in a bush, private school instead of a smart civil service job in the city with car, free housing et cetera–to give myself a certain amount of autonomy' (19). Autonomy to him is a device of *self* assertion demanding *recognition.* This unprecedented complexity which runs through the character of Odili Samalu, an idealist who gets easily disturbed by the corrupt policies of the government and is now revealed as a self seeking individual, will present an interesting contrast to the equally ambiguous Nanga who commutes between the identifications of a feigned tribal hero and a self-indulgent politician. Nanga was a Scout Master in Anata Grammar school before he joined politics. Odili, on the other hand, was an unlucky child if not a downright wicked and evil one–the bad child that crunched his mother's skull. His alienation from the world or his need for autonomy is exemplified through his own assessment and realization that 'I should have died and let my mother live.... Because it is better water be spilled than the pot broken. The idea being that a sound pot can always return to the stream' (31). This is further heightened through the hate he encounters for being the son of a District Interpreter. Thus he is not innately selfish; he is a rather precocious individual, viewing the world skeptically.

The minister's visit to Anata gives his life the much awaited turn. The recognition he receives from the Minister of Culture draws him out of his self-imposed exile and propels him. Skepticism which preceded the M.P.'s visit is blurred already. His pride thus satisfied, it becomes obligatory on his part to review his image of the former Nanga pronouncing death sentence on a highly proficient finance minister. Resolutions seem to melt under Nanga's fiery impact and he suddenly becomes a part of that country where it was said, "It didn't matter what you knew but who you knew" (19).

Odili's association with Nanga is an apt device used by Achebe to witness corruption from close quarters. Odili himself confesses: "Sitting at chief Nanga's feet, I received enlightenment. The whispers of scandalous deals in high places ... began to crystallize out of the mist. Some of the emergent forms were not nearly as ugly as I had suspected but many seemed much worse" (45). Odili is well received by Nanga. He takes him to Mr. Simon Koko without wasting much time and Odili's journey into the financial scandals and political debasement commences. The coffee which brings Koko to a near death turns out to be the product of OHMS, the brand which is sponsored by the government itself "to promote consumption of locally made the products. While the minister himself consumes Nescafe, newspaper, radio and television urged every patriot to support this great national effort" (45).

Odili, however, does not hoodwink the vast disparity existing between the power- and poverty- stricken. It so happens that in a country where the majority can afford only pails of excrement, the minister lives in a princely seven bathroom mansion with its seven gleaming silent action, water closets.

Odili recognizes that behind every proposal accepted by the government in public interest, be it the overseas training or the training of the road, there is involved a mass trading of wealth or personal interests at the higher level. Top-ranking leaders have been so immersed in the power scramble that the very essence of the post-independence democratic set up which has been strong for its own socio-cultural identity stands neglected. However, despite these instances, the luxuries associated with the political power have brushed past the idealist who now, to borrow Carroll's phrase, begins to wonder "if the world of ideals and the world of power were quite unrelated" (246). His initial detachment now transforms itself into a perspective involvement. He observes closely the professional and private life of Nanga and endeavors to give it a realistic platform.

While Nanga is alienated from the rest of the society by virtue of his improved social status resulting from the political power, Odili's academic achievement turns him into a contemptuous idealist. The crisis in all these cases lies in the fact that none of them is satisfied with his present status. It is Odili who is the worse for it. His idealism tries to counter the foreign pressure, while his exposure leaves him hankering for recognition in European circles. Achebe presents Odili as pseudo idealist, molding culture to his advantage. The flashes of insight satiate his need for recognition, while the feigned knowledge of European perception fuels his sexual desires. If we observe the novel closely, we find a subtle complexity where incidents are juxtaposed to preserve even the last ray of hope in Odili. So immediately after suggesting him as pseudo idealist Achebe takes him on a reawakening journey.

These issues serve as a window opening into the rampaging world of corruption which, despite their gravity, fails to draw any positive responses from Odili. He is excessively incensed with the luxuries associated with power. It is only when he suffers humiliation of his manliness that he reacts, but even this reaction is preceded by 'inaction' and detachment. He resents Nanga's exploit over Elsie. He himself has conveyed the impression of Elsie being a good-time girl who, indeed, she is and yet this exchange leaves him better. He, however, confronts Nanga and they depart on hostile terms. His prime concern now is to avenge himself, for Nanga had treated him as "no man had the right to treat another, not even if he was master and the other slave; my manhood required that I make him pay for his insult in full measures" (86). He intends to seek out Nanga's intended parlor wife and give her the works, 'good and proper'. In this decision of his we come across a vicious Odili here. Nanga's intended parlor wife is Edna who had caught Odili's attention since her visit to Anata as party to Nanga's entourage.

Odili combines his attraction and malignity to guarantee success to his motives which have also acquired a political objective, the C.P.C., conceived by Max and his friends. A new world unfolds for him. It is now that he learns that politics cannot be idealized; it can either be good politics or bad politics, but not ideal in the existing circumstances. Odili's return to Anata is marked by a very significant incident. He pays Edna a visit introducing himself as chief Nanga's friend. He tries to dissuade her from marrying Nanga. Thus political feud and personal vendetta proceed side by side. His decision to contest Nanga takes everybody by surprise. The quest transcends the ritualistic barrier posed by socio-cultural threats and acquires political dimensions. The society, having lost faith in itself, anticipates the arrival of a man of the people who will "comfort her and repay her for the years of shame and neglect" (91). The novel hereafter witnesses the maturing of a character. Although the former ego–the hankering for autonomy and a high estimation of himself–persists it is tempered by the extraordinary situation he is placed in. His ego is offended at the knowledge that Max was offered a higher bribe than himself to step down in favor of his rival.

Within this crisis Odili is a part of that society which, despite all its moral and cultural disorientation, still maintains, in its naivety, some of the ethical values now grossly transformed and of which it were ignorant: "If our people understand nothing else they know that a man who takes money from another in return for service must render that service or remain vulnerable to that man's just revenge" (142).

Max is an outsider striving for a political mileage. Odili is an insider who, along with his hope for European recognition, works with his mind for socio-cultural and political rehabilitation. The changes in Odili can be perceived through his frequent meditations; he sees his early idealism coming to terms with practicality which, in fact, is a response to his changing milieu. After an intellectual crisis, he rejects this in favor of the disillusioned idealism he displays at the beginning of the novel. His earlier fastidiousness guides him through disconcerting moments. It is the neglect of this finicky attitude, to some extent combined with his anxiety, that tempts him not only to attend Nanga's inaugural meeting but also confront the older man in an alien territory, unarmed and unloved.

Odili is indeed naïve in the arena of politics which is aptly represented in his secret visit to his rivals' inaugural meeting where is detected by Josiah. Josiah is the most convincing representative of the existing regime in which you see a fellow cursed in the morning for stealing a blind man's stick and later in the evening he is mounting the altar of the new shrine in the presence of all people to whisper into the ear of the chief celebrant. Odili is humiliated and severely battered when Nanga offers him the microphone jeeringly and maliciously and he sees it as an opportunity to expose him:

I come to tell your people that you are a liar and ... He pulled the microphone away smartly, set it down, walked up to me and slapped my face. Immediately hands seized my arms, but I am happy he got a fairly good kick from me. He slapped me again and again.... The roar of the crowd was now like a thick forest all around. By this time blows were falling as fast as rains on my head and body until something heavier than the rest seemed to split my skull. The last thing I remembered was seeing all the policemen turn round and walk quietly away. (157-58)

This indeed is the climax of the crisis in the novel. With the police machinery failing in a democratic set up, a military rule is clearly imminent. While Odili is in hospital after this one selfless act of attempting to expose Nanga, things worsen outside its premises. The army intervenes and disbands political parties till further notice. The quest for identity once again eludes the nation whose fate hangs in the hands of the army. The only hope which braves the dark and sinister complexity of the novel's placement is a somewhat changed Odili and a strong headed Eunice. Odili had reconciled his idealism with practicality which may eventually revert to corruption and hence stands convicted. It is Eunice in whom Achebe, after devoting the whole novel to shape Odili's character, reposes his hope and their personal loyalty unshackles all bounds to seek reprisal.

In spite of this the quest through the crisis of modern nation states still persists. Nanga's hypocrisy has been unveiled and the character denounced. Odili's disillusioned idealism and contemptuous intellectualism are mellowed by his experience in the political rivalry with Nanga. The changes in him could be perceived as practical and, perhaps, better, but with some constraint. The borrowing of funds from the C.P.C. could be the first stepping stone towards the agreement with British Amalgamated on a 'never-never' basis. His contempt for Nanga may help to preserve his identity as an educated young man who regards his cultural values (as depicted in the Max-bribing issue) and who, at the same time, is open enough to imbibe the western current only to the extent that it helps in the building of the nation as suggested by Achebe through the person of the ousted finance minister.

It is evident in the novel that western cultural invasion together with the infiltration of material luxuries is at the centre of the African confusion of identity, which poses a serious threat to cultural values. The forces of rejection, acceptance and subversion all join together at work. Amidst such confusion it is no surprise that the society loses its way. Internal resistance to the old social order now comes to the fore escalated by the foreign invasion and ruination of all chances of reconciliation and rehabilitation. Estranged from their society and alien still to the adopted culture, Nigerians, and indeed Africans, are faced with a very potent crisis—the crisis of imminent self and national annihilation. Achebe had explored this cultural and social side in his previous novels. In *A Man of the People* he gives the quest a political overtone. Should Nigeria seek recourse in Nanga, a feigned culturalist, or in the hybrid class of intellectuals? Achebe throws the ball in the readers' court; he tries to pull them out of their cynicism in order to adorn them with a strong sense of righteousness:

Overnight everyone began to shake their at the excess of the last regime, at the graft oppression and corrupt government...And these were the same people that only the other day had owned a thousand names of adulation...(166)

Achebe's voice on the identity crisis that threatens the stability of African nations is one of human protest against social injustice and tyranny, which is universal in nature and certainly transcends the borders of any cultural territory. His is an authentic African work in the sense that while on one hand it vindicates the essential validity of native cultures, it does also try on the other hand to assimilate high values from other cultures into his own scheme of things. This attitude is not one of compromise but of meaningful absorption and human togetherness.

Chapter 6

Remaking the African Myth

D Neba Che

AT the dawn of the 21st century, a few western critics still hark back to mediaeval attitudes toward the black world. They claim: "as we see (Negroes) today, so have they always been" (Wright 33) with no sense of developing beyond what nature provides them except from external (western) influence. This persistent critical cadence amongst scholars of "modern Nation States"1 is rooted in centuries of disdainful treatment of African values, in particular, and the denigration of the black world as a whole. However, foremost revisionist African mythologists like Cheikh Anta Diop2 and Chinweizu3 have successfully debunked the Western collusion in Black inferiorisation. They are joined by Ayi Kwei Armah, a dogged revisionist mythologist whose novel Osiris Rising attempts to demythologize the racist maxim that the black world is "forward never, backward ever" by resuscitating the African past as a means of restoring her lost values. This process of resuscitation, recycling and integration may not totally erase assimilated or hybrid values, for Africa owes a debt to the modern nation states and vice versa, but is simply a process of bringing into limelight what has been rejected or ignored for centuries.

Our premise is that decentering former spheres of influence gives birth to new provinces where each province has a defined autonomy enabling it to operate with little constraint within the global milieu. Although this may not allow for a protracted study of Amah's works as a whole, it traces the history of a severed continent in Two Thousand Seasons and its regenerative ability in Osiris Rising using the ancient Egyptian myth of Osiris and Isis with the intention of rebuilding the image of a vibrant Africa. In both novels Amah's proposition on the question of provincializing the modern nation states includes reconstructing or mending the dismembered past by making Africans more aware of their history.

Despite centuries of trying precisely to define Africa many a critic to date still finds it difficult to face up to the fact that Africa engendered history. Raising the ghost of 18th and 19th centuries racist philosophers and critics, for instance, the American geneticist Nobel laureate, James Watson, reopened an explosive debate about race and science with the statement that he is "inherently gloomy" about Africa's prospects in the twenty first century. "…[A]ll our social policies", he claims, "are based on the fact that their intelligence is the same as ours–whereas all the testing says not really" (qtd. in Bailey "Watson"). In another review, he contends a similar proposition:

There is no firm reason to anticipate that the intellectual capacities of peoples geographically separated in their evolution should prove to have evolved identically. Our wanting to reserve equal powers of reason as some universal heritage of humanity will not be enough to make it so. ("Watson")

This 21st century racist cadence is also espoused by no less a political leader than France's Nicholas Sarchozy in a speech delivered at the University of Cheikh Anta Diop (UCAD) in Dakar 2007 where he asseverates at length:

Africa's challenge is to enter to a greater extent into history. To take from it the energy, the force, the desire, the willingness to listen and to espouse its own history. Africa's problem is to stop always repeating, always mulling over, to liberate itself from the myth of the eternal return. It is to realize that the golden age that Africa is forever recalling will not return because it has never existed. (qtd. in Brown "Storm")

While Sarchozy's diplomatic mulling does not progress beyond the derogatory statements uttered by 18th and 19th century western racists, we may however concur on his idea of "entering history" if this entails provoking upheavals around the world: If entering history connotes arming dictatorial governments on the sly and preaching democracy on political podiums, then Africa needs to check its records; if entering history implies provoking terrorists in their closet, then Africa still needs to arm itself; and if entering history signifies owning nuclear power and preventing others from enjoying the same privilege, then Africa needs to reconsider if it really wants to join the world mafia that has transformed the globe into a terrorist battlefield–indeed, into an arena where diplomacy has become synonymous with deceit and no longer signifies an entente between nations, and where diplomacy is conditioned more by the forces of demand and supply than by any humanitarian considerations. All this 'intelligence' may be what, in Watson's view, Africa may really lack.

It is gratifying that the black world is not obliged to see the future through the western lens. Gerald Delanty in Inventing Europe: Idea, Identity, Reality contends that "the dominant ideology, the hegemon, is never entirely a monolith but is fraught with tension and contradictions", while noting that these "dominant ideas are never controlled by any single elite and can be used to subvert power" (7). The hegemon refers to a single or dominant system of thought–which is dangerous because such a system does not question its presuppositions. Like the theory of Creation, it sees its presuppositions as divinely ordained. The way out can never be the same for all nations. History remains history, be it violent or pacific, slow or fast. The process of making history varies according to the presuppositions of a people, and the circumstances at a given time and space.

The idea of a western-piloted hegemon in the making of history, sooner or later, phases out in nations beyond western frontiers, since people, time and actions are different. It is in this regard that Armah in Two Thousand Seasons and Osiris Rising views the African past as a means of redressing and − why not? − setting a new pace for remaking the history of a mutilated continent. His historiographic and mythological approaches sketch out a project for a new province by decentering former spheres of influence. His project proves that a single hegemon cannot become a yardstick for interpreting the world. Each province, while assuming its independence and identity, has the free will to borrow or not borrow from other provinces. It is only by such assertions that new centers can emerge to compete with former spheres of influence. Otherwise the process of making history will forever remain the preserve of parochial western nations imbued with the belief and conviction that they have a duty to force their values and models down the throats of non-western nations.

Armah takes his readers on a walk down the memory lane of pre-colonial, slave trade, colonial, and post independent eras in Africa with the intention of dredging up the memorable African past as evidence that the continent has made history and as justification for the prevalent chaos in the continent. By so doing, he seeks to restore the values ruined by centuries of foreign adulteration–an adulteration of which Africa cannot pretend to have totally cleansed itself because the semen is deep in the womb of the continent. These 'intruders', to borrow from Diop, Chinweizu and Armah, came from the West to divert the course of African history. Thus examining the relationship between history and literature, Amah purports that "what we call historical truth is nothing but raw material for literature...as long as historical truth is not artistically processed... it is not useful to anybody" (6). Here he sees historical truth as a commodity in a supermarket, and literature as the packaging of that commodity. If the packaging is poor, the commodity will obviously create no impact on the customer's psychology.

It is on this note that Armah carries the reader into his fictional world in Osiris Rising where, from historical and mythological perspectives, we can trace the journey of Africans to the source. Drawing the attention of his heroine to a book entitled The Journey to the Source, he sets her out on the trail of her ancestry. This journey helps expose archaeological evidence such as the "Ankh"4, the broken Ankh (the stage of betrayal), and wisdom seats like Nwt and Ama Tete, who are ready to reveal the truth about Africa through orature. In the same mould, we find such characters as Cinque ready to falsify history for self interest and Set ready to obstruct any progress. The preparatory stage of this quest is in Two Thousand Seasons where the author exposes the initial process of dismembering the continent.

Sir Harry Hamilton Johnston in A History of the Colonization of Africa by Alien Races emphasises how "the Negro, more than any other human type, has been marked out by his mental and physical characteristics as a servant of other races" (151). This contempt is not limited to the myth of servitude but is also reflected in the fact of viewing Africans as imbeciles, ferocious by nature or, simply put, as animals. Somehow these distorted images of Africa and Africans, compounded by racist theories, prompted the West and Arab traders to invade and plunder the continent, rupturing in the process the system in place. As Armah laments in Two Thousand Seasons:

They have taken everything within their reach, things that made the earth good, and they have put nothing back but hard, dead things in place of life destroyed. Even

106

their putting back has nothing of a sense of reciprocity. Their semblance of giving is parcel of their greed. It is their habit to put dead, useless things in the hollowed earth to help them take more coveted things. (7)

Armah further adds:

When the White predators from the desert came a second time they found a brood of men ready to be tools of their purpose. This time again the predators came with force to break our bodies. This time they came with guile also − a religion to smash the feeblest minds among us, then turn them as tools against us all. The white men from the desert had a discovery precious to predators and destroyers: the capture of the mind and the body both as a slave far more lasting, far more secure than the conquest of the body alone. (33)

This is part of the politics of fragmenting the pre-colonial African mind and throwing into disarray a continent that had its own way of life. The destroyer defines the people as a backward people, with little prospects for progress and advancement. Achebe and Armah draw our attention to the fact that despite the new definition of Africans, the people have their own way, which is unique to them; they are charitable, unfeigned and devoid of hypocrisy. It is this simplicity and open-mindedness that led to their undoing at the dawn of slavery and colonization. Armah christens this policy our way: "Our way is reciprocity. This is wholeness. Our way knows no oppression. The way repels destroyers. Our way produces before it consumes. The way produces far more than it consumes. Our way creates. The way destroys only destruction" (39).

If the discussion is confined to this aspect of Armah's writings, the author might be viewed merely as an apologist and a praise-singer glorifying the African past. But like the novelist Achebe, Armah's novel goes beyond the realms of propaganda to acknowledge the shortsightedness of Africans at the eve of slavery and colonization. He asserts that African history, even of the pre-colonial era, has not always been as smooth as some Africans might want to imply:

We know the society goes back not centuries but thousands of years into our past. The pattern of its life is not an unbroken line crossing the ages. It has known weakness growing to strength, vigorous life waning to suspension. At times it died. It has known birth and death and rebirth, over and again. (260-261)

It is evident from Armah's, and other significant, writing that not all the values of a past are worth saving. Even when we read the historicity behind the Ankh (the symbol of Life), we realize that the friendship of the Ankh preserved only the best of African values and its civilization. While Two Thousand Seasons appears as a preparatory exercise for the liberation of the mind, Osiris Rising clubs together the intellectual initiative for the decentering of former spheres and the eventual creation of a new Africa, which valorizes its values without ignoring its former attachment to the modern nation states. This historical process takes us on the journey by Ast (the heroine of Osiris Rising) to the roots, where she discovers the real meaning behind the Ankh after a myriad of the "Cinques" versions. The Historical Cinque, as Ast reports,

[was] an African enslaved, and taken to America. Led a revolt, took over the slave ship, [with the impression of liberating other slaves] tried to force the captain to sail back to Africa. Long story.... The story has a twist. Some sources say when Cinque got back to freedom in Africa, the neatest thing he wanted was to go into the slaving business himself. (80-81)

The Cinque syndrome is therefore the cynical attitude of distorting a people's history or way of life because of self-interest and deceit for individual ends. Cinque, Armah adds, is "one more victim turned unthinking killer, accepting the definition of freedom as dominion over others" (88). This Cinque syndrome is characteristic of the colonizers, slave traders, and the African elite, especially those who work in collusion with the west in furthering its destructive policies which consist, among others, in looking at the world through the prism of the west as the centre of the world with its "divine" hegemon. Today Africa is full of Cinques in the service of the west and their stomachs since their western counterparts constantly need their assistance to ride rough-shod over developing nations. Thus in the name of world industrialized nations, with their Janus5 faces, the west worsens the plights of developing nations in favour of transnational companies. As Oswaldo De Rivero in The Myth of Development: The Non-viable Economies postulates:

Gradually, a kind of anonymous global economic and financial dictatorship [in the name IMF, World Bank and WHO to mention a few] is being established as a result of the transnationals' lack of responsibilities in the face of unemployment, financial speculations, currency fluctuation and environmental disasters. As globalization of the market increases, democratic national control diminishes and, along with it, the feeling of belonging to a nation or a community. In this way, resignation and social anomie arise, but so do frustration and violence. In the end, the governments have turned over their domestic and international markets to the transnationals without demanding in reciprocity a joint responsibility for solving the problems that the globalization of the economy is creating. (52)

The point of this Cinque Syndrome -in a world economy where modern nation states and their transnational allies are flourishing to the detriment of developing nations—and in Amah's Osiris Rising- where the fictional character Ras Jomo Cinque Equiano and his fake Ethiopian friend falsify the history around the Ankh to crown themselves with African royalty and exploit people to satisfy their bestial ambitions—is to unmask all popular prejudice by clearly defining premises on which individuals should operate. Edward Said posits that "on the whole, it is better to explore history rather than repress or deny it" (xxvi). This unmasking process clamps down on individual egos that drive many to the periphery. Thus when Ama Tete reveals the truth behind the companionship of the Ankh that it was a symbol of life to Africans as a whole, not a matter of royalty, the revelation piques the ego of Ras Jomo Cinque Equiano and he threatens to discredit it. Cinque, together with his fake Ethiopian Prince and Set, has no other option but to hatch a plan to eliminate Asar and Ast for knowing the truth. They represent Imperialism and their transnational companies which persistently push developing nations to the periphery, and when unmasked (proven as agents of under-development, dictatorship and imperialism) and possibly sidelined, their usual reaction is to inflict economic hardships brought about by sanctions, artificial inflations and, in many cases, Western-orchestrated coups d'état. Western imperialism is to ensure that everything remains at the old centre or under the control of a single order.

The quest by Ast and Asar for true history of the people and their attempt to liberate them are thwarted by several obstacles ranging from the falsification of African history, Western interventions, African elitist obstructions and blatant murders. However, those who set off in quest of the truth will eventually succeed, as shown by the griot, Ama Tete, who narrates the plan that the ancestors had for Africa (by bringing out the symbolism behind the companionship of the Ankh) in their project of making Africa a centre for Africans. They are also satisfied to learn that their people made history but misfortune came their way and rendered many homeless in the diaspora. Amid this, the broken Ankh (symbol of betrayal) remains as a sign of home, and consequently a broken life, which can however be mended and strengthened. Knowing the truth is therefore the start of the mending process. This process of mending the dismembered Africa draws us to the myth of Osiris and Isis as parallel to Osiris Rising.

In order to resuscitate the mutilated history of Africa Armah, as a revisionist, recycles the ancient myth of Osiris and Isis and uses the analogy to prove that all is not lost; the broken values of Africa can still be restored. In World Mythology Osiris was an Egyptian savior: the chief deity of death, and the only god to rival the solar cult of Re. Sacred to him was Zedu, a town which derived its name from his fetish–several heaves placed one above the other. There, along the luxuriant waterways of the delta, Osiris was lord of the flood and vegetation as well as the king and judge of the dead. In the myth, Osiris is drowned, dismembered, and scattered over land and water by his jealous brother, Seth. The drowned one floated down the river through one of the mouths of the delta into the Mediterranean Sea and was carried to the port of Byblos. There, he was discovered by Isis, his wife and sister and daughter of the earth god Geb. Isis literally means a seat. Isis was the mother goddess of Egypt whose spittle, mixed with earth, gave life. In effect, she was also the Egyptian god of fertility. So out of envy for the happiness of Osiris and Isis arose the undying enmity of Seth who soon seized the coffin containing the dead god, cut the corpse into more than fourteen pieces, and scattered them throughout the land of Eygpt. Again, Isis sought her husband and with the assistance of Nut, the grand mother of Osiris, she resurrected the body, except his genitals: these had been consumed by fishes in the river. The reborn god, however, did not stay on earth, but became the lord of the departed in the infertile other land. Horus, the son of Isis, miraculously conceived of the dead god, was to be the avenger (40-41).

Armah parallels his plot after the above myth: Asar, the hero of his novel, is epitomised by Osiris. Like Osiris the revival god, Asar has for long been striving to resuscitate African values at the University of Manda where he is professor. Despite his efforts, the neocolonial administration in place, spearhead by his fellow brother and University mate, Set, an imperial security stooge (the embodiment of Seth), are bent on rupturing his attempts at giving identity to and liberating the University in particular and the continent as a whole from the yoke of imperialism. The timely intervention of Ast his wife, a fellow country women and classmate (the quintessence of Isis), inspired by her grand mother Nwt, (Nut's archetype) only helps grease Asar's quest for putting together the dismembered continent. Their scheme at the university materializes with the adoption of Africa-oriented curricula for History, African Studies and Literature departments. The contention begins in the University when Wright Woolley, the British head of the department of African Studies, greets the news of the imminent curriculum change with contempt: "Another Demand!" (221). His resistance is short-lived as the faculty council finally adopts the three curricula. Out of envy, Set and his entourage decide to kill Asar. Like Osiris, Asar "exploded silently into fourteen starry fragments..." (305). It is important to indicate that Asar impregnates Ast prior to his assassination. The child in her womb is Horus exemplified. Armah therefore uses this myth of rebirth as a response to the eternal western question as to whether Africa has the possibility of changing.

Since myth, as Isidore Okpweho argues, is "simply that of fancy" which informs the "creative or configurative power of the human mind in varying degrees of intensity", we can call "any narrative of oral tradition–so long as it lays emphasis on fanciful play–a myth" (19). Myth is therefore a quality that marks tales of oral tradition in proportion to their liberation from the constraints of time and experience, and this mythic quality can be identified in modern fictional works according to their indebtedness to the received material of the oral tradition in content and/or in form. Using myth in literature, Armah's intention might not be as much to parallel situations as to draw our attention to the belief that so far as Isis lives, Osiris must rise again. Isis, represented by Ast, here symbolizes the dream which Africans have of putting together their dismembered continent. It is obvious that if Osiris rises he can never be the same again since his genitals were eaten by fishes. As parts of Africa have been eaten up by slavery, imperialism, and colonialism, a new Africa can only emanate from the combination of several ancient and modern parts. It means making Africa complete inevitably entails borrowing and putting together all these parts. This further leads to the notion of building a stronger Africa by the provincializing of former spheres of influence.

As argued at the preliminary stage of this work, provincializing former spheres of influence does not mean rejecting them. The former spheres of influence have, for centuries, been the fabric of most societies around world. Chakrabarty, in Provincialising Europe: Postcolonial Thought and Historical Difference, rightly holds that

The project of provincializing Europe has to include certain particular moves: First, the recognition that Europe's acquisition of the adjective "modern" for itself is an integral part of the story of European imperialism within global history; and second, the understanding that this equating of a certain version of Europe with "modernity" is not the work of European alone; third-world nationalisms, as modernizing ideologies par excellence, have been equal partners in the process... the project of provincializing Europe cannot be a nationalist, nativist, atavistic project. (43)

From such a viewpoint, and in line with our argument, shifting former frontiers with a view to having ample space for the articulation of individual values does not entail breaking bridges, for it is only when these frontiers are shifted to a nation's favour that it can hope to achieve the great leap forward politically, socially, economically and technologically. Otherwise the tendency will always be for non-western states to constantly drift towards the eternal centre or run the risk of being swallowed in the global network created by modern nation states. Such centres will gradually grow (to the displeasure of modern nation states) to provincialize former spheres of influence thereby putting an end to the rule of the hegemon. Nations will dialogue, negotiate, rather than dictate to others. It is in this light that Asar, Ast and other colleagues adopt a curriculum at the University of Manda that places Africa at the centre with at least fifty per cent of the curriculum devoted to African Studies.

Armah's work proves that taking a progressive step entails standing by what is African more than ever amid the obstacles on the way. We also realise that hackneyed phrases on western superiority are a marketing strategy to persistently foster the western hegemon. Africans and other non-western states in order not to fall under a similar pretext should drift towards a dialogue which places each people at the centre of their activities. It is by this path that quasi nation states can, to a certain extent, avoid the error of looking at the rest of the world through the prism of western values.

Chapter 7

Culture in Fictional Contexts

AU Esimaje

THE Igbo occupy the eastern and parts of the mid-western and delta regions of Nigeria. Their area is bounded to the east by the Ibibio people and in the south-west by the Ijaw extending to the confines of Benin with Agbor as an outpost. On the northern boundary are the Idoma. There are two geographical divisions of Igbo, the riverine occupying the banks of the river Niger and the hinterland occupying the upland parts of Igboland. They are culturally homogeneous in their language of which there are nearly three hundred dialects.

Igbo laws and customs have been disrupted with the advent of colonial British government. "What now passes for native law and custom", notes Basden, "is but a travesty of what it was in the old days; it is but a shell, the kernel has been destroyed" (77). However, many customs of the Igbo have survived; one such is the culture of procreation or the love of children. Igbo literary and non fictional representations indicate that the marriage custom as it encompasses the love of children and love between husband and wife is paramount.

Marriage customs seem the foundation of the whole social structure in Igboland. Every maid or youth considers it an indispensable function to fulfil after reaching the age of puberty. In some cases female children are betrothed around such tender ages as five to seven. The notion of a celibate life finds no favour whatsoever; it is considered foolish and contrary to the laws of nature. Unlike in the Western world, traditional marriage is rather polygamous. The man needs many wives given the fact that his wife needs a long period of rest for at least three years after giving birth. So the man rightly needs many wives. Traditionally, to be the one and only wife is humiliating for the woman; it is a sure indication that her husband is poor, even wretched. A woman would rather be the head wife controlling a number of other women than a wife of no importance or authority. Polygamy invariably necessitates there being many children in the family, and what could be more desirable than that?

The Igbo further believe that he who has children is greater than he who has wealth. A man's wealth is assessed by the number of children he has, especially male children. Today, however, the polygamous tradition is waning due to westernization and the capitalist economy of postcolonial Nigeria. Yet, even within monogamy, the love for children persists.

From the foregoing, the question is often asked if Igbo traditional marriages involve love. For the African love is not closely linked with sex as with many Western races. Friendship is considered nobler than romantic love. At inception love may or may not be a feature of Igbo courtship and marriage; later something could develop, consisting of a certain degree of affection. In much earlier times, girls rarely manifested antagonism for arranged marriages. But now this submissive attitude is being superseded by the demand for liberty in the choice of a mate or husband.

Children are still of immense importance in marriage. Traditional opinions about child bearing and children show that an overwhelming majority of people–of both sexes–accept the proposition that a marriage without children is a failure. In other words, there is no family without children. A rich man who has no children is looked upon as unfortunate and unsuccessful in life: he has no sons to inherit and preserve his wealth and prosperity; his relatives, it is believed, will mismanage his wealth and property, and his wife, according to custom, is not entitled to inherit the wealth. Children themselves can even constitute a source of wealth. As Ukaegbu writes, 'This belief is reflected in the popular Igbo name "Nwa ka Ego" [children are better and superior to wealth]' (22). The works of Flora Nwapa and Buchi Emecheta have explored these themes to show how this part of Igbo culture impacts on women with its consequences for society.

Marriage, Children in Efuru and One is Enough

Flora Nwapa portrays the natural injustice and oppression which arise from childlessness. Efuru and One is Enough are relatively free of Western influence. In them, therefore, she gives her readers an in-depth description of traditional Igbo marriages. She clinically delineates Igbo customs and ends by condemning some of them. Nwapa portrays her female protagonists–Efuru and Amaka–as traditional Igbo wives in all their ramifications. They constitute appendages to their husbands although they uphold the family financially. Efuru is good at trading so she makes a lot of profit; Amaka too is good at business and makes a lot of gain. But in spite of these qualities, their husbands assume the position of lords in the house, reducing their wives to mere subordinates.

This picture accurately mirrors Igbo traditional marriages. Nwapa disapproves of this, so she creates such characters as Efuru and Amaka who are hardworking and financially independent of their husbands. By doing this, she demonstrates that the concept of a woman being a mere adjunct to her husband has nothing to do with her abilities and capabilities. In Efuru we see the protagonist rebelling against the old tradition. Efuru the heroine does this in two ways: Firstly, she arranges her own marriage which is against the tradition of paying a dowry before a marriage and, secondly, she refuses the traditional occupation of a woman in the home being farming. Describing how Efuru contracts her marriage with Adizua, the author writes:

They saw each other fairly often and after a fortnight's courting she agreed to marry him. But the man had no money for the dowry. When the woman saw that he was unable to pay anything, she told him not to bother about the dowry. They were going to proclaim themselves married and that was that. (4)

Then later, Efuru says: "If you like, go to the farm. I am not out for farm work, I am going to trade" (10). Efuru seems to assert this with a hint of authority. She does not seem to seek Adizua's approval. But soon afterwards she succumbs to the forces of Igbo tradition by accepting that she is unfulfilled without a child.

Similarly in One is Enough Amaka kicks against the Igbo tradition of marriages: she decides to stay single after her unsuccessful first marriage. In both novels, too, the heroines are driven into series of crises amidst attempts to get pregnant because of the pressures from Igbo society. The writer makes the reader aware of the humiliation of a barren woman in these words:

"I am still young, surely God cannot deny me the joy of motherhood..."
Neighbours talked as they were bound to talk. They did not see the reason why Adizua should not marry another woman, since according to them two men do not live together. To them Efuru was a man since she could not reproduce. (24)

Further in One is Enough Amaka's mother-in-law says to Amaka: "Tell me, you said I knew your plight. What is your plight? You are barren. That's all, barren ... so my son's wife, you were never pregnant, and you never will be. Get that clear in your mind" (2). In both cases, Flora Nwapa makes a conscious effort to define the role of children in traditional Igbo marriages. She does this by portraying the humiliations of childlessness and also relating the views of Igbo society through the characters in her novels. Both Efuru and Amaka contract marriages which fail primarily because they cannot have children. Thus Nwapa establishes the importance of children in Igbo marriages. Children might constitute connective and divisive factors in marriages: their presence in a home unites the man and the woman while their absence divides them.

Through Efuru and One is Enough Nwapa suggests that children actually bring honour to a woman. In essence, Igbo society places more emphasis on having children than on getting married. This is encapsulated by a character that displays disgust over the seemingly happy relationship which exists between Efuru and her husband:

Seeing them together is not the important thing. The important thing is that nothing has happened since the happy marriage. We are not going to eat happy marriage. Marriage must be fruitful. Of what use is it if your husband licks your body, worships you and buys everything in the market for you and you are not productive. (137)

This point proves axiomatic in One is Enough when Amaka's aunt says: "A marriage is no marriage without children. Have your children, be able to look after them and you will be respected" (10). Or as Amaka's mother puts it: "Marriage or no marriage, have children ... as a mother, you are fulfilled" (13).

Buttressing her claims in Efuru about the boundless importance that the Igbo culture attributes to children, Nwapa links childlessness with the worship of Uhamiri. Uhamiri, the sea goddess, is a power over and beyond everyone in the Oguta community where the novel is set. She chooses her worshippers by appearing to them through their dreams. A worshipper of Uhamiri is destined to remain childless; Uhamiri can give her beauty and wealth but not children because she herself does not have a child. Efuru is one such worshipper hence she cannot have a child. Nwapa uses this situation to show the rigidity of Igbo society and culture. Although it is widely accepted that worshippers of Uhamiri do not have children, Efuru is still expected to satisfy the demands which her society makes of all women. Nwapa seems to laugh at the disjunctiveness of Igbo culture. By placing Efuru between two values—that of Uhamiri and that of her society—the novelist shows the unyielding attitude of the Igbo and their preference of male to female children. For instance, when Efuru's daughter and only child dies, one of the sympathisers says: "…then our gods and ancestors opened your womb and you had a baby girl. We all rejoiced for you. A girl is something, though we would have preferred a boy" (72). Again in One is Enough this point is reinforced when Amaka delivers twins. Father Molaid is greatly excited when he realizes that the twins are both males: "Amaka you had twins. I am a twin myself. Oh my God, twins, both boys" (129). As a priest of God, one might expect that both sexes of children would be valued equally by Father Molaid. But his indication of a preference for male children reinforces how Igbo culture rates male children very highly. However, a female child is preferable to none.

Flora Nwapa depicts the harm these societal views of children have on society—both at the individual and societal levels. As to Efuru and Amaka, this is the root of their psychological problems. Hence at the end of the novel, Efuru becomes a sorrowful and a tragic figure because she is childless. In society the marriage institution ceases to have any significance, the presence of children being its only means of having a meaning. To make the reader aware of the utmost importance of children in Igbo culture, Nwapa introduces the culture of polygamy where the man has the right to marry as many wives as possible. The women are meant to accept polygamy, and they do. The primary aim of polygamy is to have many children. The novelist uses this to show the extent to which the men and women go in order to have children, hence the reader is not surprised to see Efuru and Amaka accept a polygamous marriage.

In One is Enough Nwapa is resolute on the importance which the Igbo attach to children. She does this by making Amaka get involved with a Catholic priest. The matching of these two people is both deliberate and symbolic. The presence of the priest is a most helpful yardstick for measuring the extent of the love for children in Igbo culture. Here are two people who are both childless: Amaka's childlessness is accidental, and the priest's by will. The priest, being sworn to celibacy, is expected to respect the institution to which he belongs. So when Amaka gets pregnant, the priest is thrown into a dilemma. He has a decision to take; he has to choose between his children and his priesthood. It appears the decision does not constitute much difficulty because Father Molaid merely says, "there are times in one's life when one is left with a choice. This is the time in my life" (109). He knows within himself that children are invaluable and should not be matched with his vow to celibacy hence he decides to leave the priesthood. He does this as a declaration of honesty. But just before he gets formally married to Amaka, he has an accident believed both by himself and his church colleagues to be a divine intervention. Consequently, he is called back to the priesthood. This shows that the love of children is generally accepted in Igbo culture.

Although Flora Nwapa condemns the degree of attachment which the Igbo attach to children, she does however accept that children should be loved and valued. She seems to be saying that children should not constitute the mainstay of marriages. Through Amaka, her spokesperson, she expresses this view:

Was that really the end of the world? Was she useless to the society if she were not married? Surely not. Why then was she suffering these indignities both from her husband and his mother? She would find fulfillment, she would find pleasure, even happiness in being a single woman. The erroneous belief that without a husband a woman was nothing must be disproved. (35)

This speech embodies Flora Nwapa's message in both novels. In effect she is saying that children and marriage are independent bodies; though one may give rise to the other, both must be valued on their own merits. It follows that a childless marriage can be happy and successful if based on love. Even a marriage which is blessed with children can be unhappy if it lacks love. Consequently, a childless woman is neither useless to her society nor unfulfilled in life.

Child Significance: Motherhood and Second Class Citizen

Through Buchi Emecheta's novels, The Joys of Motherhood and Second Class Citizen, the reader grows further aware of the great importance which Igbo culture attaches to children. Emecheta approaches the theme of the love of children in two dimensions. Firstly, she portrays the love and desire for a child as they surge in the mind of a barren woman. Secondly, she depicts the loving ways in which the mother cares for her children. In The Joys of Motherhood the reader is led through a series of physical and psychological pains which Nnu Ego, the major character, experiences because she has no child. As the novelist unfolds these fruitless efforts and sufferings to become pregnant, the importance of children in Igbo culture becomes even more apparent.

It must be noted at this juncture that productivity is culturally associated with womanhood. The ability to reproduce is almost the only connotative meaning that is attached to a woman. Such great emphasis on having a child makes the reader understand Nnu Ego's desperate desire for a child. Emecheta seems to say that in a society where much emphasis is on children, love cannot exist in its true form. So she blames the absence of love in Igbo marriages on the undue importance that the society attaches to children. She advocates a situation in which children result from a loving relationship. With The Joys of Motherhood the author clearly illustrates her claim that Igbo society places more value on children than on love. Nnu Ego reminds Amatokwu of the loving relationship between them at the beginning of their marriage. Later when their love wanes, she seeks to know the reason from her husband, and Amatokwu says:

I am a busy man. I have no time to waste my precious male seed on a woman who is infertile. I have to raise children for my line. If you really want to know, you don't appeal to me anymore. You are so dry and jumpy. When a man comes to a woman, he wants to be cooled, not scratched by a nervy female who is all bones. (32)

This speech affirms the absence of love in Igbo traditional marriages. Also in Second Class Citizen the need for children over and beyond the need for love stands out. The author writes:

Adah gaped. Seventeen good years; what did her husband do, for instance. She imagined herself in the woman's position. She tried to imagine what her life with Francis would be if she had given him no child ... she would have either died of psychological pressures or another wife would have been bought for Francis. (122)

Buchi Emecheta employs two spokesmen in her portrayal of the love of children in Igbo culture, namely, the barren woman and the woman who loves her children. In The Joys of Motherhood the author devotes a large part of the novel to the first kind of woman. She presents a captivating creation of the worries and toils the protagonist goes through in her search for children. The reader is led through series of eye-catching incidents which, even after the central character eventually experiences motherhood, are firmly imprinted in the memory. The novelist employs this art of storytelling to captivate her audience and force the reader to realize Nnu Ego's suffering. The intensity with which Nnu Ego seeks a child is clearly shown when she consents to live with a man of Nnaife's status and looks. The author conveys Nnu Ego's disappointment at seeing Nnaife thus:

...In walked a man with a belly like a pregnant cow, wobbling first to this side and then to that, the belly, coupled with the fact that he was short made him look like a barrel, his skin was pale, his cheeks were puffy and looked as if he had pieces of yam inside them ... and his clothes, Nnu Ego had never seen anything like that ... why, marrying such a jelly of a man would be like living with a middle-aged woman. (42)

However, her love for children overcomes her dislike of Nnaife hence she learns to put up with this ugly and cramped existence in Lagos.

In Emecheta's novels, events and speeches which centre on the central characters often determine their themes. They reveal the author's message and, in most cases, have dual or symbolic meanings. Emecheta's works, like all works of art, are a representation of much thought and so should not be taken merely at the literal level. The novelist's employment of duality is clearly depicted during the period when Nnu Ego finally conceives. Rather than create a picture of Nnu Ego and Nnaife making merry and thanking God because she is, at last, pregnant, Emecheta introduces conflict between Nnaife and Nnu Ego at the very moment that a conflict is least expected. And surprisingly, the effect of this is enormous. By making Nnu Ego react the way she does when Nnaife suggests keeping the pregnancy a secret, the reader is forced to follow Nnu Ego's reasoning and, at the same time, appreciate the depth of her joy. Again the author succeeds in drawing a distinction between Igbo and Western culture. Nnu Ego symbolises the totality of Igbo culture while Nnaife reflects Western ways. Nnaife who served the white masters has naturally adopted some of their ideas and ways of life. Initially he attaches less importance to children. So even when Nnu Ego becomes pregnant, he does not place the value of this child over his source of livelihood; he suggests that they make a secret of the pregnancy until they had gone to church. In Flora Nwapa's Efuru, Nnaife would be condemned for this action. For instance, when Efuru is pregnant, her friends immediately advise her to stop trading because, according to them, "he who has children is greater than he who has wealth... Money cannot go on errands" (37). In other words, a child is worth more than money. But while Emecheta's Nnaife contests Igbo culture, Nnu Ego, his wife, upholds it. To her, a child is priority; a thing of joy. Thus a sick sensation burned in Nnu Ego's head. To keep such a joyous thing secret because of "a shriveled old woman with ill-looking skin like the flesh of a pig" [Virgin Mary] (49) is incomprehensible to the traditional mother whose reaction in this instance only depicts the great love of children in Igbo culture:

She whirled round like a hurricane to face him and let go her tongue. "You behave like a slave! Do you go to her and say, "Please madam craw- craw skin, can I sleep with my wife today?" Do you make sure that the stinking underpants she wears are well washed and pressed before you come and touch me? Me Nnu Ego … if she sacks you because of that, I shall go home to my father. I want to live with a man, not a woman made man." (50)

The impression has been made that Igbo men are bossy so their wives may fear and respect them. Here the force that gives Nnu Ego the courage to talk so strongly and unflinchingly to Nnaife must be enormous. This force is the child. Emecheta portrays her talking with such strength and courage because she is the mouthpiece of Igbo society. To reinforce her claim that the child is a strong force, Emecheta introduces the reader to the new relationship that now exists between Nnu Ego and Nnaife. Since Nnu Ego has given birth, to a boy, the marriage between them experiences a consolation: "But ye see, only now with this son, am I going to start loving this man. He has made me into a real woman – all I want to be, a woman and a mother. So why should I hate him now?" (53). This speech opens the eyes of the reader to the useful role that children play in traditional Igbo marriages. By depicting the functions of children in the home, the author introduces the reader to the second image through which she explores the love of children in Igbo culture. This involves the difficulties a woman encounters in bringing up her children, which run through the second half of The Joys of Motherhood and the whole of Second Class Citizen.

The joy of having children appears incomplete until the children grow to take care of their parents. Through the process of the child's upbringing, the reader becomes aware of the problems that face the woman. By portraying the woman as she carries these problems relentlessly, Emecheta makes the reader understand that the love a mother has for her children is immense. The love of children is an inexhaustible source of encouragement to the woman. In The Joys of Motherhood Nnu Ego gives the children her unreserved attention as a mother. She devotes her whole life to them; the earlier part of her life is devoted to her search for a child, and the latter part to caring for her children. While she does this, she expects the children to reciprocate this love and also grow into dutiful men and women. This expectation is not fulfilled in the novel. Rather Nnu Ego's children fail to satisfy the yearnings of their parents: the boys grew into self-centered men, not caring for their parents. The girls kick against tradition: one of them marries into another tribe. Therefore, although Nnu Ego succeeds in having children, she remains unfulfilled in part. We can hear her say, in notes of regret, "sometimes, seeing my colleagues I wish I didn't have so many children. Now I doubt if it has all been worth it" (202). This speech shows that what the mother gets from her children at the end is not worth the pains she has taken to bring them up. One may wonder if parents must expect to gain materially from their children, yet, in Igbo culture, this material gain is one of the factors underlying the love of children.

Nnu Ego's life is best described as a long stretch of suffering. As this suffering unfolds the reader comes to realize that the joy of being a mother is not, after all, the joy of giving all to your children. Everybody has his/her own life to live. Nnu Ego becomes a typical victim of giving all to children. She gives all her life; she even sacrifices her happiness, and gains nothing in the end. The author depicts her hopelessness at the time of her death:

After such wandering one night, Nnu Ego lay down by the roadside, thinking that she arrived home. She died quietly there, with no child to hold her hand and no friend to talk to her. She had never really made many friends, so busy had she been building up her joys as a mother. And her reward? Did she not have the greatest funeral Ibuza had ever seen? Nnu Ego had it all, yet still did not answer prayers for children. (224)

Emecheta also uses the above scenario to comment on and condemn an aspect of Igbo culture. The people believe in having elaborate funeral rites; somebody may suffer throughout his whole life only to die and receive an expensive funeral. But more importantly, The Joys of Motherhood and Second Class Citizen expose the intricate relationships that exist between the institution of marriage, children and love in Igbo culture.

Conclusion

Evidently Flora Nwapa's and Buchi Emecheta's novels explore the themes of barrenness, and man-woman relationships in traditional Igbo culture but differences in their portrayals due to variation in time and place settings abound. Nwapa's novels are set in a more distant past than Buchi Emecheta's. In terms of geographical setting, Efuru is set in Oguta, a very remote village in Igboland. One is Enough has a double setting–

Oguta and Lagos–but is predominantly set in Oguta. Emecheta's novels are, on the other hand, predominantly set in the cities of Lagos and London. Hence Emecheta's novels have modern settings. Though some events take place at Ibuza, a village in Igboland, Lagos and London are very important places because the most crucial events take place there. In her novels one notices the conflict of values. This is a contrast to Nwapa's novels where one hardly hears of the formal education of children. Nwapa shows that there are many other ways through which parents can show their love for their children than sending them to school. But in Emecheta's novels the love of a mother for her children extends to her desire to see them grow into important people in society. And one way to do this is to send them to school. Thus while Nwapa portrays an ideal village life–people minding other people's business, affairs are community affairs, privacy does not exist–Emecheta gives the reader a picture of people minding their business and facing their own family problems. Consequently Flora Nwapa is closer to traditional Igbo society and people than Buchi Emecheta hence it is reasonable for readers to rely more on her stories for traditional details than on Emecheta's. Moreover, the authors employ different images to portray the love of children in Igbo culture. Nwapa creates a picture of a woman who is unable to bear children successfully. She leads the reader through the difficulties and humiliation the barren woman encounters in society. She also takes the reader through the process of the eventual joy which the woman experiences when she finally gives birth. By creating these processes she makes her reader appreciate the intensity of the love of children in Igbo culture.

To make the same statement about the importance of children in Igbo culture Buchi Emecheta adopts a different method. She places more emphasis on the rearing of the child, rather than the initial search for a child. From The Joys of Motherhood through Second Class Citizen the difficulties that Adah and Nnu Ego experience in order to rear their children amidst hard circumstances in the cities of Lagos and London are clearly shown. Through the difficulties a mother faces in educating and caring for her children, Emecheta reveals the love of children in Igbo culture.

In their portrayal of the Igbo people Nwapa's male characters are usually lazy and unambitious. Adizua, Efuru's husband, can neither farm nor trade successfully. In One is Enough Obiora does not succeed because he is not hardworking. Nwapa's men often fail because they cannot or will not work hard. Her major female characters, on the other hand, are both wealthy and industrious. In contrast, Emecheta creates male protagonists who diligently pursue their trades. Nnaife is depicted as hardworking; he avoids anything that might interfere with his work. Again, in Second Class Citizen, Francis is an ambitious and hardworking husband who fails mainly because he is not brilliant. Emecheta's female characters are not necessarily wealthy. In The Joys of Motherhood, for instance, Nnu Ego engages in petty trade which adds just a little to Nnaife's income. This difference in both novelists' portrayals of Igbo women might have come from the fact that Flora Nwapa and Buchi Emecheta hail from different parts of

Igboland, the effect of this being that they have different perceptions of their society. But theirs is indicative too that industry is not so much a feature of sex but of the individual.

The technique of both writers slightly varies; Flora Nwapa speaks through several characters in addition to the main character. These several characters comprise the entire society hence she looks through the eyes and minds of society and speaks through them. The reader learns about important messages through societal talks and gossip. This technique of speaking through society in her novel is exemplary of traditional Igbo society where a woman is expected to be humble and accommodating and to let society act as her mouthpiece. But by making characters such as Omirima and Ajanupu bear thematic messages in the novels, Nwapa, at the end, leaves the reader with vivid pictures of such characters and rather little to commend Efuru. Hence a reader unfamiliar with Igbo culture wonders if Efuru merits her position as the main character in the novel. In contrast, Emecheta speaks mostly through her main characters. When she does not speak through them, she involves them in captivating events which constitute the focus of attention. Through such dramatization Buchi Emecheta reveals her message more forcefully.

It is evident that the novels' backgrounds influence their message. Since Flora Nwapa's novels are firmly rooted in Igbo society the main characters are very much involved and owe their existence to that society. On the other hand, Buchi Emecheta makes her themes seem lighter than they really should. She achieves this by focusing on the peculiar idiosyncrasies of her central characters. The society hardly plays any significant role in their lives. By concentrating on the views of central characters, in contrast to portraying societal beliefs through many characters as Nwapa does, Emecheta gives her characters more substance and vivacity. Nevertheless, the premise that children are indispensable and act as basic necessities in Igbo marriages is abundantly clear in all their novels. In general, Flora Nwapa and Buchi Emecheta categorically reject the notion that the Igbo woman is a weak and obedient slave, a mere appendage to her man. More importantly, the novels say that children are not the primary aim of a marriage. They suggest that in marriage love should be more important than children. In exploring Igbo customs and traditions both novelists employ a peculiar realism of dealing with the relationship of love, children and marriage in Igbo culture. They inject feminine closeness into a theme that has been treated by several male writers proving that the subject of barrenness is one that may best be treated and understood in all its ramifications by a woman. Juliet Okonkwo quotes Achebe that no one understands another whose language he cannot speak (37). By exploring Igbo culture and ways of life Flora Nwapa and Buchi Emecheta have revealed the varying attitudes of Igbo women in relation to men, marriage and children thus evoking the experiences of African women in real cultural settings.

Chapter 8

Otherness in the African Novel

SA Agbor and EN Tangwa

IN postcolonial context, the term nationhood acquires significance beyond the dictionary definition of "a group of people, who believe themselves to constitute a nation, have things in common with each other and share a sense of nationhood" or as "an imaginary community where people believe themselves to have some sort of link, or commitment to others in the nation, most of whom they will never meet" (Harrison and Boyd 48). In Africa and elsewhere it is rather by the bulwark of independence struggle that the sense of nationhood was strengthened by "otherness". The relationship between the colonised and coloniser was that of the "self" and the "other" in a state of perpetual opposition. The "link" and/or "commitment that existed among the colonised in their common goal was the prime motivation for independence which was synonymous to the quest for nationhood. Harrison and Boyd go further to argue that, in order to have meaning, "nationhood... must be closely associated with the desire for self-government and the creation of a state to express that desire" (40). "Self-government" here means government by "us" and not by "them." Again this is the concept of "otherness." In other words, nationhood is a product of "otherness," Karl Deutch in Nationalism and Social Communication, asserts that "a nation is a group of people linked together by a common error about their ancestry and a common dislike for their neighbours" (75). Thus in considering the quest for independent nationhood in Africa, it is obvious that "otherness" defines "nationhood." It is true that geographical boundaries may always define a nation or the state of being a nation because if that had been the case, the nation-ness of independent African states would not have been any major concern. However, nationhood as Ortiz argues, "is not an issue of blood, nor passport, nor where you live…[it] is a condition of the soul, an ensemble of feeling, ideas and attitudes" (Morejón 970). It is the absence of this feeling, ideas and attitudes in the colonial state that led the African nationalists to seek for independence, avenue for the expression of these ideas and the self-fulfilment colonialism had denied them.

The Ghanaian novelist Ayi Kwei Armah's The Beautyful Ones Are not Yet Born (1968) may read as an allegorical story of the failure of an African ruling other Africans from colonial inherited precepts and the transformative capability of a new man emerging from the state of near-hopeless opposition. The protagonist is an anonymous railway office clerk, simply called "The Man," who struggles in the slums against poverty on one side and material greed on the other. He is pressured by his acquisitive family and fellow workers to accept the norms of society: bribery and corruption in order to guarantee his family a comfortable life. His virtues go largely unrewarded; his wife thinks him a fool. At the end of the novel, the moral strength of "the man" is contrasted to a once-powerful politician who has been deposed in a military coup. Independence in Ghana, like in most African countries becomes an avenue for a new kind of colonisation.

It is worthwhile to explore the period leading up to independence in order to determine if events at the time foreshadowed the betrayal of the African dream since independence. As to the question of what went wrong on the eve of independence, studies show that 'unpreparedness' seems to have been the key factor although the answer to this question may vary from region to region and from country to country. William Tordoff identifies this factor especially in Kenya in his book, Government and Politics in Africa:

The attempt to marry the principle of indirect Rule and Crown colony government through the inclusion in the legislature, and subsequently in the executive, of representatives of the traditional councils of chiefs came to nothing when in the 1950s it was decided to allow political parties to compete in national elections held under an expanded franchise. Thus it can be argued that the British had trained the wrong people; certainly ... meaningful preparation for independence began very late indeed and was all along rivalled and hindered by other values which were predominantly bureaucratic. (35)

This unpreparedness was not an isolated case of Kenya alone. As Bill Freud in his essay "An African Voice" notes of the hasty process of decolonisation, "the die was cast by 1951 and decolonisation began to look like a European scramble out of Africa, reversing the rapid conquest of 60-70 years earlier". Even before independence signs that the new nations would be betrayed were already visible. Yes, the colonial rhetoric of "otherness" was coming to an end; but right in the middle of the struggle, neo-colonial "otherness" was asserting itself. Writing about the case of Ghana, (the Gold Coast then) Freud notes how the UGCC, the moderate United Gold Coast Convention party mainly of the westernized elements of Gold Coast society, "favoured heightened agitation and development towards independence":

[it] stood aloof from social issues and continued all too obviously to represent the interests of the most privileged strata... [Although] Nkrumah may be taken as a model radical nationalist... the limits of his populist politics need not be considered simultaneously. At the heart of the C.P.P. affairs ... lay an ambitious core of businessmen and functionaries, less established than the U.G.C.C. stalwarts, but with similar aims and ambitions. (207)

Unfortunately these aims and ambitions were not to build a strong nation free from the chains of colonialism and economically developed as history has shown but to replace the colonialists and continue to plunder the resources of the country. In this case they were just like the independent Nigerian elite who, as the Nigerian critic Ce, notes "simply walked into the offices of their past masters and acclimatized to the status quo" (36). This view of post-independence African leaders is part of Armah's literary preoccupation in The Beautyful Ones are Not Yet Born. The nation and nationalism that Africa fought for became farfetched because it proved a new form of colonial rule. That is why Benedict Anderson in Imagined Communities believes the concept of nationalism to be imaginary; that is, a "cultural artifact." Anderson proposes a definition of the nation as "an imagined political community, and imagined as both inherently limited and sovereign" (6). He considers it imagined because a nation is made up of diverse set of people who do not know each other and yet they try to build a supposed sense of unity and develop the nation. Anderson maintains that

the creation of these artifacts towards the end of the eighteenth century was the spontaneous distillation of a complex "crossing" of discrete historical forces; but that, once created they become "modular," capable of being transplanted, with varying degrees of self-consciousness, to a great variety of social terrains, to merge and be merged with a correspondingly wide variety of political and ideological constellations. (4)

The above is applicable to post-independent Ghanaian and African societies. People's imagined sense of nationalism, as Anderson suggests, not only drives the exclusion of the "other," but also invites passion and love for one's own group or nation. The coup at the end of the novel is as a result of their continuous 'otherness' by the neocolonial leaders. The rebellion becomes a cry against their victimization and highlights the sense that a people can only be stifled for a short time but when push comes to shove rebellion becomes the outcome.

If the attainment of independence was supposed to usher in what Kevin Harrison and Tony Boyd identify as "Modern Nations" (42) William Tordoff, on the other hand, in his book entitled Government and Politics in Africa, asserts that:

Since colonial states in Africa were created within artificial boundaries—boundaries which rarely coincided with those of traditional politics—we are dealing with anti-colonial nationalism; a nationalism that was predominantly expressed within the colonial state. (47)

The result of this sort of nationalism was the attainment of independence; with independence emerged a new-found nationhood which in turn defined itself by the exclusion of the colonial other. Tordoff further argues that the birth of post-independence nations was possible thanks to the nationalists who were able to "submerge subnationalism (loyalty to a tribe or region) within a wider nationalism" (47). He goes further to state that although popular loyalties (popular nationalist sentiments) tended to gravitate towards the traditional unit —anti-colonial nationalism was able to render loyalty to a subnational unit secondary to the countrywide unit (47).

The dialectic of "self"-"other" in colonial Ghana is a source of great of humiliation and tribulation for the mass of the Ghanaian people who find themselves dwarfed to nothingness; pushed to the margin by the colonial regime which perceives the westerner as "self" and the Ghanaian as "other". This despair and sense of loss on the part of

142

the Ghanaians are vividly recaptured by Armah in the sixth chapter of The Beautyful Ones Are Not Yet Born. It has been debated that although Armah was apparently too young to take in the full import of his country's post-war social unrest–the strikes, unemployment and the shooting by the British authorities of demonstrating ex-service men recently back from the colonial war – the first twenty years of his life coincided with the growth of Ghana through a mixture of negotiation and violent struggle. No doubt Armah's creative impulse and vision have been influenced by the socio-political events of his Ghanaian society. These are the events convincingly documented in the sixth chapter of the novel in which the two characters–The Man and Teacher–provide a collective autobiography of the "new nation" and, in extension, of the independent nation-states of Africa who saw themselves as "new nations." As a critic observes:

Ghana, for instance, took the name of an old kingdom, but this was more out of romantic nationalism than any real connection with that ancient desert kingdom. In the new Ghana there would be no more Ashante, Ewe, Fante, or Ga, only Ghanaians: new nation, new people, new language, new dawn: history abolished, history starting anew. This kind of historical schizophrenia, common to all the newly independent nation-states, was not conducive to curiosity about the precolonial past beyond Negritudist celebration of culture and 'pride in our glorious past.' (Ogundele 131)

During the Second World War the British had promised the Africans freedom in case of victory. This promise thus served as a motivating force for the African soldiers who then went to war with the hope of being liberated from colonial servitude thereafter. The war ended and the soldiers returned home with high hopes of salvation at last. Armah describes the festive mood that follows this heroic historic moment in the following words of Teacher in his reminiscence:

We had gone on marches of victory and I do not think there was anyone mean enough in spirit to ask whether we knew the thing we were celebrating. Whose victory? Ours? It did not matter. We marched and only a dishonest fool will look back at his boyhood and say that he knew even then that there was no meaning in any of it. (64)

In the end, anyway, the white man fails to keep his promise and the victory the people so innocently celebrate is not theirs but his. Victory thus becomes "the identical twin of defeat" (64). Disappointment and despair return and resettle on the people, straining them to breaking point. The soldiers vent their anger on the people:

Their anger came out in the blood of those around themselves; these men who had gone without anger to fight enemies they did not know; they found anger and murder waiting for them…the land had become a place messy with destroyed souls and lost bodies looking for something that could take their anger away and finding nothing but those very people whose pain should have been their pain and for whose protection they should have learned to fight if there had been any reason left anywhere. (64-65)

Some of the soldiers like Home Boy simply find it impossible to survive the despair and go completely mad, while others "went quietly into a silence no one could hope to penetrate, something so deep that it swallowed completely men who had before been strong: they just plunged into this deep silence and died" (Armah 65). The perception of the African as "other" by the colonialist is at the root of this despair. In a society of 'self' and 'other', everything is for the self. Since the 'self' is the centre, all others gravitate around and work for the stability of the 'centre'. Being 'other' therefore, the African can be used and dumped by the colonial "master" as need be. The character, Koffi Billy, stands as a symbol of the white man's cruelty and his experience shows how profound the despair at the time is; how far it pushes the suffering people. Like any other black man in colonial Ghana, Koffi Billy can only "do work that is too cruel for white men's hands" (66). Although he does not complain, his new-found "happiness" soon costs him a leg when the English man for whom he works loads too much tension into the steel ropes and one of them snaps, cutting off Koffi Billy's leg. This "broken man" who ends up frustrated because he gets no assistance from his white employees comes to personalise the crippling effects of colonial exploitation in Ghana and Africa at large.

The despair and frustration of the pre-independence Ghanaians are not all from unemployment and economic exploitation. In fact despair has eaten so deep into their hearts and minds that the people are ready for anything as long as that thing can take them through another day of darkness and gloom. Pushed to the margin, the scenario is one of violence mixed with prostitution and other social ills as the colonised seek desperate ways and means to survive in that overcrowded margin. Sister Manaan, like many other desperate women find "refuge in lengthening bottles and a passing foreigner gave her money and sometimes love". She becomes a prostitute and an alcoholic. As Teacher puts it, the white man lives in "gleaming bungalows" on the hills away from the land that has grown "messy with destroyed souls". The African is not even worth his dog that has more meat in a day than a human Ghanaian family has in a month (66-7).

This helplessness cuts across all ages right down to the little children who are pushed by a hunger their parents cannot satisfy to go stealing mangoes from the white man's premises. Ironically, the agents of the white man's oppression are other black men who whip the hungry, desperate children "like men in the struggle for life over death" while the white man calmly watches from the hill (68). This ominous scene already foreshadows the sad realities of the dawn of independence when it seems the very thing against which they fought and died will be their lot –Africans treating other Africans as prey, as 'things' to be feared, "malins", as Naipaul writes in A Bend in the River. Although the Ghanaian society has been victimised by the white man or so-called 'master', there is nothing they can do about it, or so it seems. All they can feel is anger, but their anger is all victim-anger that had to find even weaker victims and it was never satisfied, always adding shame to itself. It is the emptiness of life around them and the prospects of an ever bleaker future that force Teacher and his friends, Koffi Billy and Sister Manaan to drug-taking; smoking 'wee' which has that effect of making their days less heavy. They believe they are the only ones with knowledge of what is happening to the Ghanaian people under colonial rule because wee lifts their natural blindness and "lets [them] see their whole life laid out in front of [them] and reveals the common facts of the waking life [they] lead. Koffi Billy's vision of his journey into the unknown "with many people going far into the distance...joined together" captures the despair and the hopelessness that has taken hold of the Ghanaian people in colonial servitude. There is no hope left in Teacher and his friend since their own people (people who ought to have stood with them against their white oppressors) have turned around and allied with the white man to oppress them and are more eager to please the white man, their master than to save their own people, just like the three black men who whip the hungry children for stealing the white man's mangoes to the satisfaction of the latter. The result is cynicism on the part of the masses that have grown tired of their "new party men".

There is thus evidence to suggest that the country is driving irretrievably towards utter disintegration. Koffi Billy is the one who first gives the impression of a lost soul in a vision when he says, "...we are going. I am just going" (74) in answer to Manaan's question, after smoking the all-revealing wee. This sense of loss and despair is further reflected in the image of the lone girl described by Teacher in the following words: "The only lonely unexplainable thing about the place was the figure of a very young girl leaning against a pole, waiting for someone no one could see…She looked more like some insect lost in all the vastness of the world around it…" (75). In the end, as Teacher puts it, it is no longer possible to "hide the knowledge of everyone's betrayal from them" (76). The post-war experience in Ghana, as Armah chronicles through Teacher's flashback, makes it crystal clear that something far more serious, far more objective and co-ordinated than individual survival tactics in that 'gloom' and 'despair' of the pre-independence era was needed to 'save' the people from colonial damnation and humiliation. The opening question of chapter six –why do we waste so much time with sorrow and pity for ourselves?–is very significant. It portrays a general sense of disillusionment. The sources of this disillusionment are well documented in this chapter of reflections and reminiscence; reminiscence of that period of colonialism during which the Gold Coast is ruled by the white men, a period of great disparity between the rulers and the ruled; the 'self' and the 'other'. Armah feels that there is an urgent need to redress the situation, to bind the masses together and claim power from the white man and build a Ghanaian nation for Ghanaians with a sense of nationhood: thus, the birth of nationalism. It is not an overstatement therefore to say that a sense of nationhood in post-war and pre-independence Africa is inspired by a sense of their own 'Otherness', a sense of their nothingness under the colonial master. Armah himself points out this disparity between the whites and the blacks, the humiliation and marginalisation of the Ghanaian, when Teacher observes that "water coming from the hills [where the white men live] was always clean, like unused water, or like water used by ghosts without flesh" (67). Something thus has to be done to retrieve the marginalised from the margin and place them on a level of equality with everyone else; to give them that sense of belonging of which they have been so long deprived by colonialism.

Though based on a period of over ten years, The Beautyful Ones Are Not Yet Born seems to cover merely a few days of hopelessness with only one flashback. This 'blast from the past', presented in the sixth chapter of the novel is invaluable in revealing the causes of the decay, the deprivation and the poverty with the state of dystopia that Armah describes so explicitly. It is this poverty, deprivation and great inequalities between the so-called 'Rulers' and 'Ruled' in this state of dystopia made real in Ghana and elsewhere in Africa by colonialism that spurs a coterie of Gold Coast intellectuals whose primary objective (at any rate, from the outset), is to awaken in the masses that sense of nationhood; the only tool they have and which they can use to take power from their oppressor. Initially high hopes and expectations meet the arrival of the intellectuals who pose as 'saviours' of the people. After the decades of humiliation in the margin, such reaction from the Ghanaians can only be expected. At last "something new [is] being born". So the "voices when people spoke now were a little loud" (76). But Armah is quick to point out the futility of these dreams. The only reason, Teacher says, that can explain the loud voices, is "the ridiculous hope that false happiness would reassure the desperate" (76). And truly these first men are far from reassuring to the people because as earlier noted, they are more interested in pleasing their master, the white man than in serving and 'saving' their own people from the white man. The people therefore grow weary, half hopeful, half sceptical and half embarrassed by these men who claim to hold the key to a brighter future for them. As Teacher puts it:

Many things happened then which we ourselves had no way of understanding. Strangers, our own people who had gone as seamen to the West Indies came back wearing only calico and their beards, talking openly of the white man's cruelty. We all said they were mad, of course, but if you stood with one of them long enough and listened to his words without too much fear...it would become very hard for you to tell on which point exactly the man was mad. And so people feared them...for the disturbing, violent truth of some of the things they were so often saying. (76)

This shows that there has been a silent acceptance by the Ghanaians of their subaltern status under the white man because they fear him; that is why they regard these new men who come telling them that they are equal to the white man with fear for what Teacher calls their "violent truths". Had these men not been less hypocritical in their condemnation of the white man, they might have succeeded in rallying the people behind them. Yet despite their gentleness and courage in challenging the position of the white man, the new men still fail to get the support of the people to build a Ghanaian nation free from colonial rule. The reason for their failure is a simple one: they fail in their struggle to reject the white man against whom they claim to fight and the people are quick to realise this.

If the struggle was a struggle for nationhood, a nation to which all belong on equal grounds, for such a nation to emerge, the white man, the colonial master who does not envisage any equality between black and white, between 'self' and 'other', must be rejected and ejected from the country so that the long marginalised Africa can leave that contemptible margin and occupy their rightful place in the 'centre.' Thus these promises and plans of salvation prove deceitful when these same men who have hitherto rejected the white man in order to satisfy the hopes of "big and beautiful things" are found to be scrambling to welcome the white man on their backs. The people however know that for any change to be genuine their leaders must come from the marginal group, people who would be ready to reject the white man, not those "trying at all points to be the dark ghost of a European", speaking to their servants in legal English, talking of constitutions and offering unseen ghosts of words and paper held holy by Europeans and yet claiming to be the "magicians" of the people. As Armah asks, how were these leaders to know that while they were climbing up to shit on their people's faces their people had seen their arseholes and drawn away in disgusted laughter? (82).

Armah's novel shows what the politicians fail to know, but which the people know very well, and that is "the only real power a black man can have will come from black people". It is only such power (it is hoped) that can look on all black people as equals, as people with some dignity, in fact, as humans and not the sub-humans to which colonial bondage had reduced them. And so the

151

people gradually and steadily lose hope in their flatulent politicians and their "Plan R. Plan X. Plan Z." and all curiosity about the "old men wanting to be new leaders" dies (82). In the end, it was Nkrumah who sought to retrieve his people from the margin and bring them to the "centre" to reclaim power from the white man and build a nation of their own through independence. However, this was a non-peaceful and highly controversial process. In Ghana and elsewhere in Africa as noted earlier, the transition to independence and nationhood in Africa was marked by both violent struggles and peaceful negotiations. Everywhere it was black men rising to lead their people out of colonial subordination to "freedom and equality." But few Ghanaians like Teacher in The Beautyful Ones Are Not Yet Born are sceptical of these "new old layers" who want to "share" power with white men watching over them. Armah admits nevertheless that if the demeaning colonial policies were thorns in the flesh of Africans, they did at least have something positive for the continent albeit for a relatively brief spell: they forced the different and previously mutually hostile ethnic groups bundled up together during the Partition, to submerge their national identities under the National identity and thus stand in 'brotherhood' and fight and "defeat" the white man. "United we stand; Divided we fall" was the maxim, and the "new man" must take advantage of it and make a difference, unlike his predecessors who had stood aloof from the people posing as "saviours" or "magicians" with "some secret power behind them".

Yet looking at the post-colonial situation in Africa of endemic otherness in modern nation states as identified in

Armah's novel, the question of nothing has changed at all in Africa still remains. Have the goals which pushed Africans to such "crimes" and "sacrifices" in their quest for nationhood been attained? Or was nationhood just a mirage? Armah uses sordid imagery and symbolic language of narrative in The Beautyful Ones Are Not Yet Born to show that nationhood is a farce in Africa and that the much celebrated independence does not in any way make Western 'otherness' a thing of the past; that the great idea of the oneness of the African peoples against the colonial, oppressive, repressive, and exploitative European regimes was nothing but a ploy that only served and yet continues to serve the interests of a select parochial few who remain the sordid legacy of Western civilisation in Africa.

Chapter 9

Nationalism in the African-dictator Novel

MK. Walonen

MUCH has been made critically of the Latin American literature of dictatorship which comprises, among other texts, such magisterial works as Gabriel Garcia Marquez's The Autumn of the Patriarch (1975) and Mario Vargas Llosa's The Feast of the Goat (2000). Considerably less attention has been paid to the similarly rich sub-Saharan African literature, found particularly within the genre of the novel, which has exploded over the past four decades or so as a means of interrogating the rise of autocratic regimes across the continent in the years following the downfall of the various colonial orders that had previously held sway. Sources of amusement and/or dread for onlooking world audiences, of adulation and/or detestation for their own people, the specters of African dictators continue to haunt the continent and its body of cultural production.

The postcolonial African dictator was invariably a product of the Cold War and the relative social instability and state of economic underdevelopment that reigned in the wake of the vast colonial pullout--grudging or well intentioned as it may have been in individual cases--of the nineteen fifties and sixties1. Mobutu Sese Seko in 1965, Muammar al-Gaddafi in 1969, Mengistu Haile Mariam in 1974... these figures rose to power via coups d'état, overthrowing the fragile democracies and monarchies that had succeeded colonial rule. They were generally propped in place, financially and/or militarily, by the CIA, laboring under domino theory anxieties, or the U.S.S.R., looking to spread the dictatorship of the proletariat (though losing the qualifying prepositional phrase contained in that expression in the process). Their politics of oppression, cult of personality, human rights violations, and administrative corruption defined an era in African history, one lasting roughly from the late sixties until the end of the Cold War--though in some cases these dictators rule up through the present day, and in almost every case their legacies of poverty and brutality endure within the countries they governed with iron fists. Accordingly, the literature they inspired, with its interrogation of the dynamics of worldly power and the possibilities of resistance to it, occupies a central place in the world of African letters from the the nineteen seventies well into the twenty-first century.

The current vogue in the humanities is to analyze the more subtle, indirect functioning of power. Contemporary critical theory has fueled this trend, from Louis Althusser's notion, first explored in "Ideology and Ideological State Apparatuses: Notes Toward an

Investigation," of the ideological state apparatuses that complement the more direct repressive state apparatuses in enforcing control, to Michel Foucault's conceptualization of the diffuse nature of power in modern society:

Power must be understood in the first instance as the multiplicity of force relations immanent in the sphere in which they operate and which constitute their own organization: as the process which, through ceaseless struggle and confrontations, transforms, strengthens, or even reverses them; as the support which these force relations find in one another, thus forming a chain or a system, or on the contrary, the disjunctions and contradictions which isolate them from one another; and lastly, as the strategies in which they take effect, whose general design or institutional crystallization is embodied in the state apparatus, in the formulation of the law, in the various social hegemonies. (92)

These insights have contributed to a bevy of incisive analyses of the subtle functioning of power and control spread throughout the complex, highly stratified industrial and postindustrial societies of the recent past. But when it comes to societies in which power has a much more blunt and brutal face this attunement to power as something diffuse and systemic is not necessarily in order.

Literary commentators, native African and non-native alike, have sought to come to terms with the complex interplay of repression, patriarchal authority, tribalism, nationalism, residual colonial power structures,

Afrocentrist and/or third world socialist rhetoric, and so forth that undergirded the regimes of African dictators during the late Cold War period.

There are multiple potential points of textual entry into the literary interrogation of this social phenomenon, notably Chinua Achebe's Anthills of the Savannah (1987), Wole Soyinka's A Play of Giants (1984) and Giles Foden's The Last King of Scotland (1998). our study shall focus on V.S. Naipaul's A Bend in the River (1979), Ngugi wa Thiong'o's Wizard of the Crow (2006), and Nuruddin Farah's trilogy Variations on the Theme of an African Dictatorship—Sweet and Sour Milk (1979), Sardines (1981), and Close Sesame (1983). Each of these texts offers an incisive perspective on the social-psychological dynamics of authoritarianism, how dictators maintain power, and the living conditions of ordinary individuals under modern despotic regimes. Taken together, they offer a range of ideological perspectives, from the conservativism of Naipaul through the feminism of Farah and the populism of Ngugi; a range of ideas regarding how to create more egalitarian and democratic societies in Africa; and a range of geographic focuses, from Naipaul's Congo through Farah's Somalia and Ngugi's dystopian synthesis of a number of sub-Saharan African states.

While Naipaul, Farah, and Ngugi by no means exhaust all there is to be said in reference to the postcolonial dictatorships of Africa, A Bend in the River, Wizard of the Crow, and Variations on the Theme of an African Dictatorship expand the literary critical discourse devoted to achieving a greater understanding of the predominant political system manifested in postcolonial Africa.

V.S. Naipaul's novel A Bend in the River is a thinly veiled critique of Mobutu Sese Seko's regime in 1970s Zaire, a fictionalized version of the observations and reflections Naipaul offered earlier in his Congo Diary (1980) and his essay "A New King for the Congo: Mobutu and the Nihilism of Africa" (1975). It narrates the experiences of narrator/protagonist Salim, an East African of Indian Muslim extraction, as he moves to an unnamed central African country closely based on Zaire, earns a living as a shopkeeper, has an extended affair with the wife of a politically influential university historian, and watches the country slide further and further into social instability under the brutal and repressive regime of a dictator referred to simply as 'the Big Man.'

In "A New King for the Congo" Naipaul had already charted out much of the thematic territory pertaining to how "Big Men" of Mobutu's ilk achieve power: the dictator achieves his position of power by way of a mixture of revolutionary rhetoric and appeals to patriarchy, virility, and, strategically, the ideas of both old Africa and new Africa (91).

The African dictator maintains this power, according to Naipaul, by tapping into the traditional authority invested in the figure of the chieftain, by projecting an air of unpredictability that keeps his subjects constantly on edge, by keeping his followers cognizant of the fact that he can suddenly return them to the humble social status from which he raised them to positions of wealth and influence, and because for his subjects obedience is an effective means of warding off despair over their disempowered and degraded situation (64, 95, 126).

A Bend in the River dramatizes this order of things through such oppressive measures enacted by the Big Man as his nationalization of businesses owned by non-Africans, his use of the Youth Guard to terrorize and humiliate the civilian population, his capricious use of national resources like the country's main passenger airliner, his trumpeting of a mythic sense of Africanness via such means as replacing a statue of a European explorer with one of a spear-wielding African tribesman, and his fostering of a legal system rife with corruption, where statutes like the interdiction against trading in ivory tusks are selectively applied as means of extortion.

Numerous commentators have pointed out the obvious shades of Conrad's Heart of Darkness in Naipaul's fictional Congo, and certainly the Big Man offers a version of Kurtz's megalomania even further enabled by a greater degree of control over human and material resources made possible by the circumstances of his time and geopolitical situation. But cutting across his evocation of the politics of oppression is Naipaul's rather racist imputation to the Congolese of a constitutional unfitness to occupy roles requiring advanced technological, mercantile, and/or administrative roles in a complex society. This, plus the violence and social instability that become increasingly pronounced as the text progresses, leads to a rampant sense of anxious unease among the African population of A Bend in the River that in turn produces a will to destruction and a desire to return to the primitivism of "the bush."2

Ranu Samantrai posits in his "Claiming the Burden: Naipaul's Africa" that in the logic of the novel Africans are infantilized vis-à-vis more 'adult' and 'mature' individuals of European and Asian descent, and as such the Big Man's efforts to modernize the nation and to assert himself as a strong, independent leader are efforts to deny and cover up his intrinsic African childishness and underdevelopment:

[I]n the Africa of Naipaul's imagination [...] [u]nder the benevolent rule of the colonial father, there was a safe place for the exercise of the feminine/ maternal power of the bush. The bush was developed wisely, never violated. At its heart it remained a safe haven for African men, a separate sphere where they could remain children [...] Colonial Africa was a world in which there was a well-ordered place for everyone, and everyone knew his/her place. Paradoxically, when the men of Africa rebel against the rule of the father in the name of the mother [mother Africa, symbolically embodied in the text in the venerated figure of the Big Man's mother], they destroy this stability. The very man who gained the confidence of Africans by promising to sanctify the mother and her terrain tries to "bypass the real Africa" (108) by imposing modernity on the bush. (59)

So in A Bend in the River the dictator steps into the breach left in the wake of the European father's disappearance, a child parading in the raiment of an adult, engaging in inauthentic measures and lacking the maturity to show discretion, govern wisely, and temper his cruel tendencies.

Like Naipaul, Nuruddin Farah sees the social dynamics of oppression and dictatorship as an extension of a family dynamic that equates paternity with absolute authority and command. In an interview with Patricia Alden and Louis Tremaine Farah states that dictators proceed ineluctably from the basic fabric of their society, which is an outgrowth of the family unit (30). In an interview with Kwame Anthony Appiah he remarks that the supreme self-confidence of dictators and their inability to listen are essentially a paternalistic masculine trait (58). Throughout Variations on the Theme of an African Dictatorship, Farah's three volume fictional exploration of General Siad Barre's decades-long autocratic regime in Somalia, the manner in which the father as absolute ruler of the Somali family provides a model and justification for the virtually unlimited power of the dictator. In the words of Wilhelm Reich, which Farah quotes as an epigram to the first volume of the trilogy, Sweet and Sour Milk: "In the figure of the father the authoritarian state has its representative in every family, so that the family becomes its most important instrument of power" (103).

Sweet and Sour Milk tells the story a dentist, Loyaan, who attempts to uncover the circumstances leading to the death of his recently deceased twin brother, Soyaan, a government adviser who has been clandestinely involved with a small group of Mogadishu's intellectual elite working to resist the ruling dictatorship3. The father of the pair, Keynaan, is a petty tyrant in his own right, trying to regain the favor of the regime—which he lost after inadvertently killing a man he was torturing in his

161

former position as a police inspector--by posthumously claiming Soyaan as a martyr of the General's 'socialist revolution.' In a symbolically loaded image Loyaan repeatedly recalls a scene from his youth in which his father takes away a ball illustrated with a map of the world that the two brothers have been fighting over and tears it in two (17). Here Keynaan is not only presented as "The Grand Patriarch [who] rules, with the iron hand of male-dominated tradition, over his covey of children and wives" (55), but as a force of violent division and separation--separation into the paternal symbolic order of sharply differentiated subjectivity, not to mention a force of wanton destruction of carefree childhood fancy. Moreover, Keynaan's proclamation as he cuts the ball in two–"A world round as a ball. Whoever heard that?"–marks his action as a triumph of flat-earth unimaginative traditionalism backed by force and convention-based authority over the spirit of imagination and exploration. "I am the father," Loyaan imagines his father saying through this act later in the text, "It is my prerogative to give life and death as I find fit [. . .] if I decide this minute to cut you in two, I can. The law of this land invests in men my age the power. I am the Grand Patriarch" (102).

Sardines, the second volume of Variations on the Theme of an African Dictatorship, shows that these forms of patriarchal authority and control are not vested solely in the persons of the older generation of Somali men, but are spread across the institutions of Somali society. The plot of the novel centers on Medina, an independent, intellectual woman who has moved out of the house she previously shared with her husband,

Samater, due to the fact that he has been coerced into accepting a position as a government official and that his mother, Idil, has moved into the house and begun threatening to have Medina's daughter Ubax circumcised. Medina herself has already had this process performed upon her, both literally/physically as a young girl and figuratively, in the sense that she has recently been silenced when stripped of her position as editor of the country's only daily newspaper following her refusal to publish government propaganda. The potential clitoridectomy of Ubax represents the disempowerment of women and the younger generation in the Somali society of the novel, not to mention the preempting of a rich and full life for each as well. Female circumcision is equated with paternalistic control, as the text further illustrates through its reference to a Somali-American couple whose American-born daughter was seized by tribesmen and forcibly circumcised. Medina exercises all efforts in her power to prevent this from happening to Ubax, and thus, symbolically, to maintain the promise of a better, less oppressive future for Somalia.

In contrast with both Sweet and Sour Milk and Sardines, the final volume of Farah's trilogy, Close Sesame, offers a vision of a benign, understanding patriarch not principally motivated by a desire for power. Close Sesame narrates the story of Deeriye, a devout Muslim who has achieved the status of local hero due to having been imprisoned for a considerable amount of time by both the Italian colonial regime and the postcolonial dictatorship of "the General," as he balances the possibilities of violent political resistance against his ethical proclivities towards nonviolence, all in the face of the winnowing down of his son Mursal's underground opposition group due to a series of failed assassination attempts. Deeriye serves as a foil for most of the fathers in Close Sesame, particularly Xaaji Abraham, who takes his patriarchal power and command so far that he kills his son for standing in opposition to the General's regime. In contrast, Deeriye is an understanding father who neither controls nor meddles in the affairs of Mursal and his sister Zeinab. Through the figure of Deeriye Farah shows that the role of the father does not need to be one of absolute authority and rule, even if this is the traditional mode of paternity in Somali society. Nonetheless, Close Sesame points out that the formative influence of the father, even a liberal and non-controlling one, is inevitable. In a conversation later in the novel Deeriye and his brother-in-law, Elmi-Tiir, reflect that even if Deeriye was away in prison for most of his son's upbringing, he still provided the heroic "myth" that guided Mursal's development, eventually leading him down the path of resistance to the General and, consequently, his death (237).

Patriarchs exist in Variations on the Theme of an African Dictatorship not just on the top of the social pyramid in the person of the dictator and at the base in the form of literal fathers but also in the intermediary figure of the chieftain. Even though these three novels take place in the urban setting of Mogadishu and its environs, the rules and kinship connections of tribal society still predominate, and as such tribal chiefs exert just as pronounced a role in determining the rule of law, custom, and punishment as the other incarnations of patriarchy in Farah's work. Throughout the trilogy the

General takes advantage of this social structure to consolidate his power, using tribal elders to enforce obedience, particularly among the younger generation, and pitting tribes against each other as they jockey for favorable position under his regime.

Beyond their role in maintaining compliance with the status quo, the various patriarchal structures sounded out in Variations on the Theme of an African Dictatorship exert a profound influence on the process of identity formation. As Patricia Alden and Louis Tremaine argue in their book-length study, Nuruddin Farah, a recurrent theme in Variations on the Theme of an African Dictatorship is the manner in which the individual autonomy which is necessary for self discovery is imperiled by the oppressive dynamics of patriarchal control:

Farah's protagonists recognize that their autonomy is threatened, not by a single dictator but in multiple and complex ways [. . .] [t]hey undergo an education into the nature of power as a system and, in particular, the interconnections among dictatorship, patriarchy, and colonialism; they recognize that this system of oppression operates by taking control of available social formations (family, clan, state, religious and ideological communities) and, consequently, that these formations and indeed all social relationships must be critically examined and may need to be resisted or transformed. (94)

So what is at stake in this process of examination and resistance is a fight against forces which would not just circumscribe or delimit individual lives, but also the entire process of individuation capable of producing agents with the capacity to resist these various forms of oppression in the first place.

Perhaps the most central way that the dictatorial regime of Variations on the Theme of an African Dictatorship works to co-opt identity formation is through its manipulation of signifiers of identity. During the period in which Sweet and Sour Milk and Sardines are set Somalia was aligned with the Soviet block, from whom it received substantial aid, and thus General Barre professed that his government was an embodiment of Marxist-Leninist revolution. In the early pages of Sweet and Sour Milk, before he dies, Soyann gives lie to this pretension, calling the country "fake socialist [...] but really fascist Somalia" (16). Later the text notes that the soi-disant socialist General's political affinities run far more to the extreme right as he warmly receives such strong-armed African dictators of the era as Gaddafi, Idi Amin, and Jean-Bédel Bokassa (97-98). As Amin, Malak argues in his "Dissecting Dictators: Nuruddin Farah's Close Sesame," Farah's General hollows out such popular-appeal-laden labels as "Marxist-Leninist" and "Islamic" as a way of garnering consent and legitimizing his rule (48).

Another Orwellian sleight of hand perpetrated by the General, as Alden and Tremaine point out (92), is his falsification of history as a means of cementing his power. After Soyyan's death in Sweet and Sour Milk he is co-opted as a hero of the General's revolution who died with words of praise for the dictator upon his lips, despite the fact that he has been working underground in opposition to the regime, writing tracts denouncing it. As a state functionary remarks to Loyaan, "They are re-writing your family's history, Soyaan's and the whole lot. Like the Russians rewrote Lenin's, Stalin's or that of any of the heroes their system created to survive subversion from within or without" (115). Creating a pantheon of mythic heroes is a time-honored tradition of autocratic regimes looking to maintain support by trumpeting the values they purport to embody --from the Nazis and Horst Wessel to the cult of African womanhood that Zaire's President Mobutu fostered around the figure of his deceased mother. Beyond this, controlling a sense of the past serves both as a means of influencing a populace's sense of national identity and presenting a sense of what is possible or impossible in the present.

All told, in its manipulations of language and fact, the General's regime presents a form of cultural hegemony that largely precludes effective large-scale resistance to its reign. By controlling an operative sense of social reality and the horizons of the possible/conceivable, autocratic regimes enforce consent just as effectively as through more direct repressive means. As Farah puts it in his article "Why I Write," "dictatorial regimes [...invest] power more in their own variety of truth, each of which [has] a fictive truth to support its validity, than in the plain home-grown truths you and I grow in our (fertile?) imagination" (9-10).

Through its use of forms of ideological control Farah's dictatorship goes beyond the means of control enacted by the Italian and British colonial regimes in Somalia but, at the same time, it draws upon some of strategies of direct repression handed down from the colonial era as well.

Margaritta, Soyaan's former lover, reflects in Sweet and Sour Milk that after the heady years of optimism and postcolonial democracy of the 1960s: "Came the '70s. Army coups. Barefaced dictatorships. We see Africa 'taken back' to an era she had lived through before, the era of European dictatorship, concentration camps. Africa is again a torture-chamber. Africa is humiliation" (134). "Are you saying that Africa is the same or nearly the same torture-chamber as it was when the colonials were here?" Loyaan asks in reply, "Or are you saying that African dictatorships are but a re-creation of the same methods and things these career-soldiers learned from their colonial masters during the toughest struggles?" (135) She replies somewhat ambiguously, implying that there is some truth to each of these alternatives: "Or something like that" (135).

The same basic sentiment is expressed by Deeriye in Close Sesame: "when Africa attained its political independence, black apes took over and aped the monkeys who trained them" (102). The mode of life that prevails within these oppressive social orders so uncannily reminiscent of colonial rule is one of desperate elation and widespread delusion: "what dictatorships are or create [… is] [m]ass madness. Mass euphoria" (138). It is one of secret police, illiterate bands of loyal youth 'Green Guards,' de facto compulsory mass assemblies in praise of the ruling general, and midnight arrests and brutal interrogations. It is one Loyaan, summing up the net result of the forms of social oppression Farah's trilogy surveys, bluntly describes as "a prison" (210).

In its first few pages Ngugi wa Thiong'o's comic magnum opus, Wizard of the Crow, tips its proverbial cap to Variations on the Theme of an African Dictatorship, referring, as Sweet and Sour Milk does, to a wife of the novel's central dictator figure who is punished for a transgression by being stuck perpetually in the same moment: clocks frozen in time, the same food served day in and day out, and the same radio and television programs played over and over (8). In each novel this episode illustrates the dictator's godlike conceit of trying to stop or go outside of time, an impulse which recurs later in Wizard of the Crow when the dictator, known as the Ruler, reaches the culmination of his megalomania in attempting to 'abolish' the future and inaugurate an eternal present in his country (750-751).

Wizard of the Crow narrates two stories, at times parallel, at times intersecting: that of the Ruler of Aburiria, a fictional African country, as he attempts to acquire funds from 'the Global Bank' to build as a testament to his power a modern day Tower of Babel, and that of Kamiti and Nyawira, a man and woman who stumble on the role of faux wizard as a means of evading the police, and then find themselves beseeched by a procession of people looking for magical intervention including, eventually, the Ruler himself. Along the way, it offers an intricate analysis of how dictators acquire and maintain worldly power and of how the changing geopolitical dynamics of the past two decades have forced dictators to adapt in order to retain their positions of control.

Wizard of the Crow leaves the circumstances surrounding the Ruler's rise to power shrouded in hearsay and uncertainty, noting that many competing "stories are told" (231). Only one of these, however, is delineated: that, in the manner of the likes of Bokassa and Amin, he won favor during the late colonial era through servile and accommodationist behavior. Like Mobutu he abandoned a career in journalism for the greater prospects of advancement military life offered, and like numerous African dictators he shortly seized power from the first post-independence president of the country (231-233). Once in power, the Ruler keeps himself in place by currying the favor of the West and controlling the military and the nation's natural resources, both of which he places in the hands of his dissipated sons (9, 645). He also manages to negotiate what Okolo points out as the paradox of dictatorship, of concentrating so much power in the hands of a single individual: that it can only be accomplished through relying on others (63). The Ruler manages this state of things by repeatedly creating new orders and appointing new ministers to consolidate his hold over the country and then replacing his ministers and/or pitting them against each other to preclude their own construction of a formidable power base (230-231, 702).

Moreover, the Ruler stays in power by such direct repressive means as police surveillance and the pursuit of dissidents, as well as by controlling what is accepted as knowledge and historical fact. As the text progresses the Ruler extends his sway over basic semantics, dictating that "sorcerers, diviners, [and] witchdoctors" will "be called specialists in African psychiatry, in short, afrochiatrists" and that "[i]nstead of using the word past [Aburirians] would talk about African modernity through the ages, and they should talk of the leading figures in Africa's march backward to the roots of an authentic unchanging past as the great sages of African modernity" (622).

Ngugi's novel offers a compelling perspective on how authoritarian regimes in Africa may have become more subtle with the changing times, but by no means less oppressive and exploitative. In doing so, he reminds us that, though the dictators of the nineteen seventies and eighties sketched by Naipaul and Farah have either disappeared like Mobutu or adapted like Gaddafi, most African nations are no closer to attaining participatory government and a higher standard of living. In fact, as Adebayo Adedeji points out in his article "An Alternative for Africa," the severe forms of austerity imposed on debt-ridden African nations by the World Bank and the International Monetary Fund have brought about a considerable rolling back in any gains in quality of healthcare, education, and infrastructure achieved during the early postcolonial era (119). Adedeji has gone on to argue that to ameliorate this situation it is necessary to turn to indigenous African solutions to the crises facing the continent, particularly returning to pre-colonial localized consensual forms of government rather than continue to mimic "the Western model of divisive political parties" (126).

Thus the turn from continued forms of totalitarianism or their residual to more participatory forms of government is to be attained by a return to organically rooted rather than exogenous political forms. Whether this or any other currently proposed mode of reform will prove to be viable means of addressing the debilitating

legacy of both colonialism and the more recent bloody
history of African dictatorship remains to be seen.

Notes and Bibliography

Chapter 1
Global Flows

Notes

1The term 'twice migrant' was first used (1985) by Parminder Bhachu in her book Twice-Migrants East African Sikh Settlers in Britain to refer to Indian migrants who relocated to Britain from Africa.

2Personal communication. October 2002.

3Jhatka is a quick jerky movement in Bollywood dancing and matka means a seductive swaying movement that has become incorporated in the vocabulary of Bollywood viewers and journalism.

4Personal communication. May 2008.

5Larkin's mention of a similar audience in Kano, Nigeria who would stand for three hours to watch Hindi films when tickets to the open air theatre were sold out confirms the popularity of Hindi films in different parts of Africa where films like Mother India ran for decades (Npg).

6Personal communication. Nair states that their [of people in Senegal, Cameroon, Gambia and many parts of Francophone Africa] "memories petered out with the India of "Sholay". Still, a TV Channel in Dakar obligingly telecast "Lagaan" dubbed in French to convince the sceptics amongst the disbelieving Indians there that Hindi cinema still held its own" (2004 Npg).

7A paper he presented at the CSA Conference in 2008

Works Cited

Bhachu, Parminder. Twice Migrants: East African Sikh Settlers in Britain. Tavistock, London and New York, 1985.

Chakravarty, Sumita. National Identity in Indian Popular Cinema, 1947-1987. Austin: University of Texas Press, 1994.

Devadas, Vijay. 'Cinema in Motion: Tracking Tamil Cinema's Assemblage.' Paper presented at "From Bombay to LA: The Travels of South Asian Cinema." Asia Research Institute, National University of Singapore (9-10 Feb 2009).

Derne, Steve. Movies, Masculinity and Modernity: Ethnography of Men's Film Going in India. Greenwood Press: Westport. 1999.

Ebrahim, Haseenah. "From "ghetto" to Mainstream: Bollywood in South Africa. Scrutiny2, 13, 2. 2008 (63-76).

Fair, Laura. "Making Love in the Indian Ocean: Hindi Films: Zanzibari Audiences, and the Construction of Romance in the 1950s and 1960s." Love in Africa. Ed. Jennifer Cole & Lynne M Thomas. Chicago: University of Chicago Press, 2009.

Larkin, Brian. "Bollywood Comes to Nigeria." Samar 8: Winter/ Spring, 1997. 31 March 2010 <www.samarmagazine.org/archive/article.php?id=21>

_ _ _. "Bandiri Music, Globalization, and Urban Experience in Nigeria." Social Text - 81 (22, 4), Winter 2004 (91-112).

_ _ _. Indian Films and Nigerian Lovers: Media and the Creation of Parallel Modernities. In The Anthropology of Globalization: A Reader. Jonathan Xavier Inda and Renato Rosaldo eds. Oxford: Blackwell Books. 2002.

_ _ _. "Itineraries of Indian Cinema: African videos, Bollywood and Global media." Multiculturalism, Postcolonialism and Transnational Media. Eds. Ella Shohat and Robert Stam. New Brunswick: Rutgers University Press. 2003 (170-192).

Machado, Pedro. "Threads that Bind: South Asia, Africa, and Cloth Zones of Contact in the Indian Ocean in the 18th and 19th Centuries." Cultural Studies Association Conference. NYU May 2008.

Mishra, Vijay. Bollywood cinema: temples of desire. Routledge, New York and London, 2002.

Nair, Janaki. "View from Africa." The Hindu. Sunday, September 26 2004.   31st   March   2010. <http://www.hindu.com/mag/2004/09/26/stories/2004092600010050 0.htm>

Prasad, M. Madhava. Ideology of the Hindi film: a historical construction. Delhi; New York: Oxford University Press, 1998.

Ray, Manas. "Chalo Jahaji: Bollywood in Diaspora – in the Tracks of Indenture to Globalization." City Flicks. Ed. Preben Kaarsholm. Seagull, 2004 (138-179).

_ _ _. "Bollywood Down Under: Fiji Indian Cultural History and Popular Assertion." Floating Lives: the Media and Asian Diasporas. Ed. Stuart Cunningham and John Sinclair. USA: Rowman and Littlefield, 2001 (136 – 184) .

Rush, Dana. "The Idea of "India" in West African Vodun Art and Thought." India in Africa: Africa in India: Indian Ocean Cosmopolitanisms. Ed John Hawley. Bloomington: Indiana University Press. 2008.

Tharoor, Shashi. "Why Nations should Pursue Soft Power." TED Talk. March 31 2010. <video.i-newswire.com/shashi-tharoor-why-nations-should-pursue-soft-power/-United States>

vander Steene, Gwenda. "Hindu" Dance Groups and Indophilie in Senegal: The Imagination of the Exotic Other." India in Africa: Africa in India: Indian Ocean Cosmopolitanisms. Ed. John Hawley. Bloomington: Indiana University Press, 2008.

Chapter 2
African Spaces, European Places

Works Cited

1Conquering the body of a people is an easy conquest. Yet, the conquest of the mind is a continual battle and conquest is not as readily attainable. The colonial powers in Africa conquered people but native, cultural imperatives prevailed in most cases.

2Africans, in exile 'within' and 'without' their homes, retain cultural imperatives and an 'oral' linguistic heritage as evidenced in the writings of Chinua Achebe, Wole Soyinka, Aminatta Forna, and Donato Ndongo.

3Aminatta Forna's Sierra Leonean heritage, not British heritage, assumes a primary position in her writings.

4'Extended memory' is a reference to a 'Collective memory' which stems from the 'collective I'. It is not restricted to one individual. It is a communal memory spanning over various times and spaces, within the African cosmology.

5The dialogue and/or intercourse between the characters are not restricted to a specific time frame.

6F. Abola Irele (2001) reviews this issue in his text. Dr. Sasha Johnson, in the text of her dissertation (2008), addressed the relationship between identity (for Africans and African-Americans) and language for African-Americans.

7Johnson (Linguistics) discussed, in consultation for this paper, the plausibility of a transfer of primary, inherent linguistic tendencies upon written language. She concluded that her research lead her to believe that such a transfer could occur. (*November 2009)

8Aminatta Forna's step-mother is acknowledged by the author as having taught her Temne, the language of her Sierra Leonean father, over one summer. However, Forna was absorbed in the 'oral' culture and traditions of the Temne language long before she mastered speaking the language itself.

9Syl Cheney-Coker's masterpiece The Last Harmattan of Alusine Dunbar is a 'break-out' work for Sierra Leonean, African Realism. The protagonist embarks upon an allegorical, cosmic journey that transcends several time periods. The author is, also, able to interpose African-American, African and colonial history with the metaphysical and the ontological. This work was critically acclaimed by Wole Soyinka.

10Tempels theories regarding the Bantu people and their religion may have been 'generalized' by the Catholic Church to marginalize all African, religious beliefs. His theories prevail in some circles today.

11Donato Ndongo extends the range of the 'collective I' in a fashion that enhances it. The 'collective you' becomes an extended range for the author to speak 'to' and 'from' his people. In doing so, the author often admonishes himself and his people at times.

12African Realism is different from the Western, literary element 'Realism'. African Realism is exclusive to the African, cosmic experience.

13Complementary Realism is another term for African Realism by the Nigerian scholar, Emezue, who in a recent study of Chinua Achebe's Anthills of the Savannah and Chin Ce's The Visitor argues that "a more valid conceptualization of African reality from a complementarist paradigm is that which presents ... a world where all life interacts – the unborn, the living, the dead, the ancestors, the past, the present, the good, the bad – in a seeming endless cycle of existence powered by choices." (238)

14Donato Ndongo must refute the dogma of the Catholic Church before he can reclaim his true African identity.

15The elders of Equatorial Guinea assumed a highly, prestigious role in grooming and training the young men to become men versed in the traditions of the tribe.

16Donato Ndongo's saga continues in the books which follow Shadows of Your Black Memory.

Works Cited

Achebe, Chinua. Things Fall Apart. New York: Ballantine Books, 1959.

Booker, M. The African Novel in English. New Hampshire: Heinemann, 1998.

Coker-Cheney, S. The Last Harmattan Of Alusine Dunbar. Hampshire: Heinemann International Press, 1990.

Connolly, Cressida. "Notches on the wheel." 2 July, 2006. 7 November, 2009. <http://www.telegraph.co.uk/culture/books/3653678/Notches-on=the-wheel.html>

Emezue, GMT. "Complementary Realism: Achebe, Ce." New Black and African Writing Vol. 1. Eds C. Smith and GMT Emezue, AI: African Books Network, 2009. 237-360.

Evita, Leoncio. Cuando Los Combes Luchaban. Madrid: Agencia Espanola De Cooperacion Internacional, 1996.

Forna, A. Ancestor Stones. London: Bloomsbury Publishing, 2006.

Hanson, S. "The chaos of politics, 4 mesh in Africa," Atlantic Monthly Press 1 October, 2006. 7 November, 2009 <http://www.sfgate.com/cgi-bin/article.cgi?f=/c/a/2006/10/01/rvgfqldqug1.dtl&type>

Irele, F. A. (2001). The African Imagination. New York: Oxford University Press, 2001.

Iweala, U. "As It Really Was." nytimes.com. 24 September, 2006. 15 November, 2009 <http://www.nytimes.com/2006/09/24books/review/Iweala.t.html?sq=aminatta>

Homer, The Odyssey. Trans. Robert Fagles. New York: Penguin Press, 1966.

Imbo, Samuel. An Introduction to African Philosophy. Maryland: Rowman & Littlefield Publishers, 1998.

Johnson, S. R. "Acknowledging The Voices Of Families: Metadiscourse And Linguistic Identity Of African American Speakers Of AAE." Doctorial dissertation, University of Georgia, 2008.

Lewis, M. An Introduction to the Literature of Equatorial Guinea: Between Colonialism & Dictatorship. Missouri: University of Missouri Press, 2007.

Masolo, D.A. African Philosophy in Search of Identity. Indiana: Indiana University Press, 1994.

Mukherjee, N. "Stories Woven into a Tissue of Truth." Times Online 24 June, 2006. 16 November, 2009, <http://entertainment.timesonline.co.uk/to/arts_and_entertainment /books/fiction/article67

Ndongo, Donato. Shadows of Your Black Memory. Chicago: Swan Isle Press, 2007.

Ngamba, Monique. "Common features and Particularly in Five Black African Postcolonial Novels In European Languages: Default; Darkness of Your Black Memory, The House Gun; Une Vie De Boy And O Desejo Kianda." Tonos Electronic Journal of Studies Filologicos, December 2004. 9 November, 2009. <http://www.um.es/tonosdigital/znum8/estudios/15-monique.htm>

N'gom, M. Dialogos Con Guinea. Madrid: Labrys 54 Ediciones, 1996.

− − −. "La autobiografia como plataforma de denuncia en Los poderes de la tempestad, de Donato Ndongo-Bidyogo." Afro-Hispanic Review Spring 2000, October 9, 2009 (66-71).

− − −. "La Literaturea Africana de expression castellana; La creacion literaria en Guinea Ecuatorial," Hispania, September, 1993. 9 October, 2009. <http://www.jstor.org/stable/343796>

Okri, Ben. Astonishing the Gods. London: Phoenix House, 1995.

Parker, P. "Rocks and a hard place," The London Times Online. 23 July, 2006. 16 November, 2009. <http://entertainment.timesonline.co.uk/tolarts_and_entertainment /books/fiction/article68>

Shahriari, S. "Exiled from Equatorial Guinea, a visiting professor awaits the time he can return home." 11 May, 2008. 9 November, 2009, <http://www.columbiamissourian.com/stories/2008/05/11/hoping-home-exiled-equitorial-guinea>

Shilling, J. "Tracing the patterns of the past," Telegraph. 6 July, 2006. 7 November, 2009. <http://www.telegraph.co.uk/culture/books/3653676/Tracing-the-patterns-of-the past.html>

Todorov, T. The Fantastic: A Structural Approach to a Literary Genre. Cornell University Press, 1973.

Virgil. The Aeneid. Trans. Christopher Cranch. New York: Hachett Publishing.

Wheelwright, Julie. "Aminatta Forna 'We don't commit suicide – we kill'". The Independent. 30, June, 2006. 7 November, 2009. <http://www.independent.co.uk/.../aminatta-forna-we-dont-commit-suicide--we-kill-406003.html

Chapter 3
African and AmerIndian Epistemologies

Works Cited

Abrams, David. The Spell of the Sensuous. New York: Vintage Books, 1997.

Anzaldua, Gloria. Borderlands/La Frontera: The New Mestiza. San Francisco: Aunt Lute Books, 2007.

Díaz-Polanco, Héctor. La Rebelión Zapatista y la Autonomía. Coyoacan: Siglo Veintiuno Editores, 1997.

Dussel, Enrique. "Eurocentrism and Modernity." Boundary 2 20:3, 1993. 64-76.

Emezue, GMT. "Complementary Realism: Achebe, Ce." New Black African Writing: A Critical Anthology Vol. 1. Ed. Charles Smith and GMT Emezue, AI: African Books Network, 2009. 237-60.

Grants, Amanda. "Memory, Transition and Dialogue: The Cyclic Order of Chin Ce's Ouevres." Journal of African Literature. 3, 2006. 11-29.

Howe, LeAnne. Shell Shaker. San Francisco: Aunt Lute Books, 2001.

– – –. "The Story of America: A Tribalography." Clearing a Path: Theorizing the Past in Native American Studies. Ed. Nancy Shoemaker. New York: Routledge. 2002. 29-48.

Mariátegui, José Carlo. Seven Interpretive Essays on Peruvian Reality. Austin: University ofTexas, 1971.

Mignolo, Walter. Local Histories/ Global Designs: Coloniality, Subaltern Knowledges and Border Thinking. Princeton: Princeton University Press, 2000.

Mignolo, Walter. The Darker Side of the Renaissance. Ann Arbor: University of Michigan Press,   2003.

Ngugi wa Thiong'o. Matigari. Harare: Zimbabwe Publishing House, 1987.

Ogaga, Okuyade. "'Locating the Voice': The Modernist (Postcolonial) Narrative Maze of Chin Ce's The Visitor." Critical Supplement (A)1: The Works of Chin Ce. Ed. Irene Marques, IRCALC. 2007. 135-157.

Quijano, Anibal. "Modernity, Identity and Utopia in Latin America." Boundary 2 20:3 (1993), 141-1 55.

Chapter 4
The Ancestral Diaspora

Notes

1 See Daryll Cumber Dance, From my People: 400 Years of African American Folklore (New York: Norton & Company, 2002) 507, and Joseph M. Murphy, Working the Spirit, 147.

2 Caribbean poet Kamau Brathwaite pays homage to the remnants of history some would prefer to forget: not a fabled Africa, as Dayan asserts, but the spirits who are born out of the stresses and tortures of the flesh. See Joan Dayan, "Who's Got History? Kamau Brathwaite's 'Gods of the Middle Passage,'" World Literature Today 68 (1994): 726.

3 Vincent Brown, The Reaper's Garden: Death and Power in the world of Atlantic Slavery (Cambridge: Harvard UP, 2008) 261.

Works Cited

Baucom, Ian. Specters of the Atlantic: Finance Capital, Slavery, and the Philosophy of History. Raleigh-Durham, Duke University Press, 2005.

Bigsby, Christopher. "The Ground on which he Stood." The Cambridge Companion to August Wilson. Ed. Christopher Bigsby. New York: Cambridge UP, 2007. 1-27.

Brown, Vincent. The Reaper's Garden: Death and Power in the world of Atlantic Slavery. Cambridge: Harvard UP, 2008.

Dance, Daryll Cumber. From my People: 400 Years of African American Folklore. New York: Norton & Company, 2002.

Dayan, Joan. "Who's Got History? Kamau Brathwaite's Gods of the Middle Passage." World Literature Today 68 (1994): 726-732.

Dezell, Maureen. "A 10-Play Odyssey Continues with Gem of the Ocean." Conversations with August Wilson. Ed. Jackson R. Bryer and Mary C. Hartig. Oxford: University Press of Mississippi, 2006. 253-256.

Drewal, Henry John. "Mami Wata and Santa Marta: Imag (in)ing Selves and Others in Africa and the Americas." Images and Empires: Visuality in Colonial and Postcolonial Africa. Ed. Paul Stuart Landau and Deborah D. Kaspin. Berkeley: University of California Press, 2002. 193-211.

Elam, Harry J. The Past as Present in the Drama of August Wilson. Ann Arbor: UP Michigan, 2006.

Freedman, Samuel G. "A Voice from the Streets." New York Times on the Web 15 March 1987. 10 November 2009 <http://www.nytimes.com/1987/03/15/magazine/a-voice-from-the-streets.html>.

Furman, Jan. Toni Morrison's Fiction. Columbia: University of South Carolina Press, 1996.

Glissant, Édouard. Poetics of Relation. Trans. Betsy Wing. Ann Arbor: UP Michigan, 1997.

Gordon, Avery. Ghostly Matters: Haunting and the Sociological Imagination. Minneapolis: University of Minnesota Press, 1997.

Hanchard, Michael. "Black Memory Versus State Memory: Notes Towards a Method." small axe 26 (2008): 45-62 .

Murphy, Joseph M. Working the Spirit: Ceremonies of the African Diaspora. Boston: Beacon Press, 1994.

Opoku-Agyemang, Kwadwo. Cape Coast Castle. Accra: Ghana, Afram Publications, 1996.

Patterson, Orlando. Slavery and Social Death: A Comparative Study. Cambridge: Harvard UP, 1982.

Philip, M. NourbeSe. Zong!. Middletown: Connecticut, Wesleyan UP, 2008.

Powers, Kim. "An Interview with August Wilson." Conversations with August Wilson. Ed. Jackson R. Bryer and Mary C. Hartig. Oxford: University Press of Mississippi, 2006. 3-11.

Roach, Joseph. Cities of the Dead-Circum-Atlantic Performance. New York: Columbia UP, 1996.

Rushdy, Ashraf H. Remembering Generations: Race and Family in Contemporary African American Fiction. Chapel Hill: UNC Press, 2001.

Shannon, Sandra G. The Dramatic Vision of August Wilson. Washington, D.C.: Howard University Press, 1995.

Wilson, August. Joe Turner's Come and Gone. New York: Penguin, 1988.

___ ___ ___. Gem of the Ocean. New York: Theatre Communications Group, 2006.

___ ___ ___. The Ground on Which I Stand. New York: Theatre Communications Group, 1996.

Chapter 5
Modernity and African Identity

Works Cited

Achebe, Chinua, A Man Of People. London, 1966.

Anand, Mulk Raj. Untouchable. London: Wishart, 1935; New York, New York Liberty Press, 1935.

Bernth, Lindfors. "Achebe's African Parable." Critical Perspectives on Chinua Achebe. Ed. Bernth Lindfors and C. L. Innes. Washington DC: Three continents Press, 1978.

Bhattacharya, B. So Many Hungers: Delhi: Orient Paperback, 1978.

Ce, Chin. "Igbo Mind, Music, Culture and Religion (I)." Riddles and Bash: African Performance and Literature Reviews. Oxford: African Books Network, 2010.

− − −. Trilogy: Children of Koloko, Gamji College, The Visitor. AI: Handel Books, 2008.

Gareth, Griffith. "Language and Action in the novel of Chinua Achebe." Critical Perspectives on Chinua Achebe. Ed. Bernth Lindfors and C. L. Innes. Washington DC: Three Continents Press, 1978.

Singh, Khushwant. Train to Pakistan. London: Grove Press, 1956.

Soyinka, Wole. The Interpreters. London: Heinemann, 1984.

Wa Thiong'o, Ngugi. "A Man of the People." Critical Perspectives on Chinua Achebe. Ed. Bernth Lindfors and C. L. Innes. Washington DC: Three continents Press, 1978.

− − −. Homecoming: Essays on African and Caribbean Literature, Culture and Politics. London: Heinemann 1972.

− − −. Weep Not, Child. London: Heinemann, 1964.

Chapter 6
Remaking the African Myth

Notes

1The great western industrialized powers who claim the responsibility to create a new international order. This is opposed to quasi nation-states (needing to develop).

2 C. A. Diop's two books, Nations negres et culture (1954) and Anteriorite des civilizations negres (1967), have profoundly influenced thinking about Africa around the world. It was largely because of these works that, at the World Festival of the Arts held in Dakar in 1966, Dr. Diop shared with the late W. E. B. DuBois an award as writers who had exerted the greatest influence on Negro thought in the 20th century.

3In the great tradition of twentieth century black emancipation movements Chinweizu's seminal book publication in 1975, The West and the Rest of Us: White Predators, Black Slavers and the African Elite, proves a damning exposition and indictment of centuries of western racism revisionism.

4A symbol of the strong, productive and united African past

5An old Italian deity represented with two faces looking different ways.

Works Cited

Armah, Ayi Kwei. Two Thousand Seasons. London: Heinemann,1979.

__ __ __. Osiris Rising. Popenguine: Per Ankh, 1995.

Brown, Karimo "Storm Over Mbeki's Letter to Sarkozy" 23 August 2007.
<http://www.business.co.za/article/topstories.aspx?=bd4A546272>

Bailey, Ronald. "Is Nobelist James Watson, Co-Discoverer of the Structure of DNA, a Racist?" October 16, 2007
<http://www.reason.com/blog/show/123028.htlm>

Chakrabarty, Dipesh. Provincialing Europe: Post Colonial Thought and Historical Difference. Princeton: Princeton University Press, 2000.

Cotterrel, Arthur. A Dictionary of World Mythology. Oxford: Oxford U P, 1979.

Delanty, Gerard. Inventing Europe: Idea, Identity, Reality. London: Macmillan, 1995.

De Rivero, Oswaldo.The Myth of Development: The non-viable economies of the 21st Century. London: Zed Books, 2001.

Hegel, George Wilhelm. The Philosophy of Histories. Trans. J. Sibree. New York: Dover, 1956.

Johnston, Harry Hamilton. A History of the Colonization of Africa by Alien Races.Cambridge: Cambridge University Press, 1905.

Okpewho, Isidore. "Rethinking Myth" in African literature Today N0 11, ed.Eldred Jones. London: Heinemann,1980: 15 – 23.

Said, Edward W. Culture and Imperialism. New York: Vintage Books, 1993.

Wright, Michel M. Becoming Black: Creating Identity in the African Diaspora. Durham: Duke University Press, 2004.

Chapter 7
Culture in Fictional Contextx

Works Cited

Achebe, Chinua. Morning yet on Creation Day. London: Heinemann, 1975.

Basden, George T. Niger Ibos: A description of the primitive life, custom and animistic beliefs of a little known African people. London: C & SS, 1966.

Emecheta, Buchi. The Joys of Motherhood. London: Heinemann, 1979.

Emecheta, Buchi. Second Class Citizen. London: Fontana / Collins, 1974.

Nwapa, Flora. Efuru. London: Heinemann, 1966.

Nwapa, Flora. One is Enough. Enugu: Tana Press, 1981.

Okonkwo, Juliet I. 'The Talented woman in African Literature', African Quarterly, Vol. XV, No 1, 1975.

Ukaegbu, Alfred O. Marriage and Fertility in East Central Nigeria: A case study of Ngwa Ibo woman, Ph.D Thesis, University of London, 1975.

Chapter 8
Otherness in the African Novel

Works Cited

Anderson, Benedict, Imagined Communities. London: Verso. 1991. Print.

Armah, Ayi Kwei. The Beautyful Ones Are Not Yet Born. London: Heinemann, 1968. Print.

Behrent, Megan. "Ama Ata Aidoo: Independence and Disillusionment in Postcolonial Ghana." Scholars.nus.edu.sg (Web).Thursday, 8th June 2006.

Ce, Chin. "Bards and Tyrants: Literature, Leadership and citizenship issues of modern Nigeria." African Literary Journal, B5 (2005): 3-24. Print.

Dandala, Mvume. "A Call to Harness the Spirit of the Nation". Journal of Theology for Southern Africa. Web.uct.ac.za (Web). May 2004

Deutch W. Karl. Nationalism and Social Communication: An Inquiry into the Foundations of Nationality. New York: John Wiley& Sons, Inc. 1953. Print.

Freud, Bill. The Making of Contemporary Africa: The Development of African Society Since 1800. London: McMillan, 1984. Print.

Harrison, Kevin and Tony Boyd. Understanding Political Ideas and Movements.Manchester: Manchester University Press, 2003.

Mbile, N.N. Cameroon Political Story: Memories of an Authentic Eye Witness. Limbe: Presbyterian Printing Press, 1999. Print.

Morejón, Nancy. "Transculturation, Translation, and the Poetics of the Caribbean" Callaloo 28.4. (2005): 967-976 . Print.

Naipaul, Vidiadhar Suraiprasad. A Bend in the River. New York: Random House, 1979. Print.

Ogundele, Wole. "Devices of Evasion:The Mythic versus the Historical Imagination in the Postcolonial African Novel." Research in African Literatures, 33.3 (2002): 125-139. Print.

Tordoff, William. Government and Politics in Africa. London: McMillan, 1997. Print.

Igwe, Leo. "African Humanism: A Vision of Hope and Renewal". Humanist Visions for Africa. Iheu.org (Web). 27 June 2005.

Chapter 9
Nationalism in the African-dictator Novel

Works Cited

Anderson, Benedict, Imagined Communities. London: Verso. 1991. Print.

Armah, Ayi Kwei. The Beautyful Ones Are Not Yet Born. London: Heinemann, 1968. Print.

Behrent, Megan. "Ama Ata Aidoo: Independence and Disillusionment in Postcolonial Ghana." Scholars.nus.edu.sg (Web).Thursday, 8th June 2006.

Ce, Chin. "Bards and Tyrants: Literature, Leadership and citizenship issues of modern Nigeria." African Literary Journal, B5 (2005): 3-24. Print.

Dandala, Mvume. "A Call to Harness the Spirit of the Nation". Journal of Theology for Southern Africa. Web.uct.ac.za (Web). May 2004

Deutch W. Karl. Nationalism and Social Communication: An Inquiry into the Foundations of Nationality. New York: John Wiley& Sons, Inc. 1953. Print.

Freud, Bill. The Making of Contemporary Africa: The Development of African Society Since 1800. London: McMillan, 1984. Print.

Harrison, Kevin and Tony Boyd. Understanding Political Ideas and Movements.Manchester: Manchester University Press, 2003.

Mbile, N.N. Cameroon Political Story: Memories of an Authentic Eye Witness. Limbe: Presbyterian Printing Press, 1999. Print.

Morejón, Nancy. "Transculturation, Translation, and the Poetics of the Caribbean" Callaloo 28.4. (2005): 967-976 . Print.

Naipaul, Vidiadhar Suraiprasad. A Bend in the River. New York: Random House, 1979. Print.

Ogundele, Wole. "Devices of Evasion:The Mythic versus the Historical Imagination in the Postcolonial African Novel." Research in African Literatures, 33.3 (2002): 125-139. Print.

Tordoff, William. Government and Politics in Africa. London: McMillan, 1997. Print.

Igwe, Leo. "African Humanism: A Vision of Hope and Renewal". Humanist Visions for Africa. Iheu.org (Web). 27 June 2005.

Printed in the United States
By Bookmasters